Praise for
JEFF BARTSCH

"Jeff is one of the most talented and trusted editors I have ever worked with. I think anyone considering the opportunity to learn from Jeff should leap at the chance."
– *Frank Sinton, Executive Producer/COO A. Smith & Co. Productions, Former VP Programming FOX Sports Net, Former VP Programming Disney Channel*

"When I want to captivate and wow an audience, I turn to Jeff. And if you are serious about telling stories that resonate powerfully with your audience, I recommend you do the same."
– *Jan Landis, 8-time EMMY-winning Television Producer, Dr. Phil/ABC/TV Guide Network*

"Editors are a dime a dozen – Jeff is an artist. The difference is that Jeff doesn't just tell a story, he makes you FEEL it."
– *Mary Jaras, Executive Producer/Showrunner, A&E, VH1, MTV, FOX, NBC, E!*

"Working in a variety of genres, Jeff's use of music, effects, and pure instinct makes the raw elements of picture and sound come alive."
– *Anthony Storm, Vice President/Executive Producer, A. Smith & Co. Productions, ESPN, UFC, FOX Sports Net, TV1*

EDIT
BETTER

HOLLYWOOD-TESTED STRATEGIES
FOR POWERFUL VIDEO EDITING

©2014 by Jeff Bartsch

All rights reserved. Except as permitted by the U.S. Copyright Act of 1976, no part of this publication may be reproduced, distributed, or transmitted in any form or by any means or stored in a database or retrieval system without the written permission of the publisher. Any use of the information in this book is at the sole discretion of the reader, and the author and publisher specifically disclaim any and all liability arising directly or indirectly from the use of the information contained in this book.

Published by Resolve Entertainment, Inc.

Cover design: Gordan Blazevic
See Gordan's portfolio at www.99designs.com, designer OberonZG

Interior layout: David Paprocki
See David's portfolio at paprocki.squarespace.com
Author photo: Stephen Busken, www.buskenstudio.com

Resolve Entertainment, Inc.
24307 Magic Mountain Parkway, Suite 350
Valencia, CA 91355
Info@ResolveEntertainment.com

Printed in the United States of America

To learn more about powerful communication through video editing, connect with the author and like-minded individuals at:

www.ThePowerEdit.com
www.Youtube.com/user/thepoweredit
On Facebook, look for "The Power Edit" and "The Power Edit on FB."

First edition 2014, first printing

ISBN-10: 0-9904325-0-5

ISBN-13: 978-0-9904325-0-0

WARNING!

If your reaction to the title of this book is something along the lines of "Okay, tell me more," or "Sweet!!" …then you're gonna love this.

If your reaction to the title of this book is some variation of "Who does he think he is?" or "How *dare* you?!"…this book will likely drive you nuts, and I'd hate for you to suffer unnecessary mental pain.

EDIT BETTER is filled with ideas and rules, and like the art of editing, every rule has an exception. Sometimes a whole bunch of them.

This book is not about telling you what to do. It's about providing a jumping-off point for you to **do your editing the way you want to**.

It is not exhaustive or complete on any subject it addresses. You would not want to read a book that is – that book would be 927 pages long and dry as burnt toast.

It will not tell you which editing tools to use. It does not tell you what the buttons do on your favorite editing software – in fact, this book studiously avoids discussion of the specific tools of editing – the rest of the world is happy to dive into the details of that.

What this book offers instead is a wide-ranging overview of the creative application of video editing. These ideas apply whether you're telling your story with the latest fancy software, or with filmstrips, scissors, and a roll of splicing tape.

EDIT BETTER is targeted at the advanced hobbyist and emerging or growth-minded professional, toward the vast majority of the creative world who edits projects that are not – and do not need to be – multi-million dollar movies, as sexy as that idea may seem. There are plenty of books that fully discuss the intricacies of film editing. This is not one of them.

Instead, this book offers real-world, boots-on-the-ground, Hollywood-tested strategies and ideas to help your editing and your projects communicate clearly, effectively, and powerfully.

In short, **BETTER**.

Many a video, film, or TV editor has worked with directors, producers, or clients who know that something about the edit isn't working, but just can't put their finger on what it is. In frustration, they finally ask, **"I don't know, isn't there a button to just make it better?"** No matter how much the editor might hunt for the **BETTER** button, it can't be found… because it doesn't exist, and it never will.

This book exists to help you *become* the ever-elusive **BETTER** button.

CONTENTS

WARNING! ix

INTRODUCTION xix

Why this book?
Who are you?
Who am I?
Assumptions… and your editing

THE TELESCOPE AND THE MICROSCOPE 1

Tactics vs Strategies

PART 1 – THE TELESCOPE 5

THE THREE HATS OF THE EDITOR   7

Technician
The Creative
Psychologist: The Boss, Audience, and Self

THE IMPORTANCE OF EDITORIAL PLANNING   19

Rule #1: Determine your Desired Outcome.
Rule #2: Determine your Message.
Rule #3: Determine your Market.
Rule #4: Determine your Media.
Rule #5: Determine your Method.

PART 2 – THE MICROSCOPE   49

EDITORIAL STRUCTURE   51

Rule #6: Understand the piece before you begin editing.
Rule #7: When in doubt, start with what you know to be important.
Rule #8: Put your structure into visual form.
Rule #9: Find the backbone of your piece and hang everything on it.
Rule #10: Put your main pieces in place before adding anything fancy.

GENERAL RULES FOR EDITING   61

Rule #11: Read Walter Murch's *In the Blink of an Eye* to understand why editing works at all.
Rule #12: Actively direct the viewer's attention.
Rule #13: Guide the viewer's eye with sequential attention magnets.
Rule #14: Show what *is* by contrasting with what is *not*.
Rule #15: Seek simplicity by highlighting only what's important.
Rule #16: Be aware of what you're explaining and what you're not.
Rule #17: Play peek-a-boo with your audience by use of The Reveal.
Rule #18: Be willing to enter a scene already in process.
Rule #19: Consider editing backwards.
Rule #20: Be willing to experiment.

THE SINGLE EDIT 83

Rule #21: Begin a shot just before an action begins, leave when the action ends.
Rule #22: Use pauses in audio or dialog to trigger cut points.
Rule #23: Be aware of on-camera subjects blinking when cutting.
Rule #24: Put your edit point exactly on the beat of a music track only if you want to emphasize the edit itself.

TRANSITIONS: Getting from Here to There 93

Rule #25: Think of transitions like you're writing a novel.
Rule #26: Minimize the use of fancy digital transitions.
Rule #27: Make sure the transition doesn't step on anything it shouldn't.
Rule #28: Stretch your creativity to make ideas flow without visual crutches.

MUSIC: Select, Place, and Arrange 103

SELECT
Rule #29: Treat music as a character equal to anything or anyone in your piece.
Rule #30: Factor in expectations when selecting music.
Rule #31: When in doubt, choose music that exaggerates your piece's existing emotion.

PLACE
Rule #32: Decide whether the music is acting or reacting.
Rule #33: Use music to begin, end, or change ideas.

ARRANGE
Rule #34: Fit the music to the piece, not the piece to the music.
Rule #35: Alter the music most effectively by preserving established patterns.
Rule #36: Leave markers on music changes, hits, or energy shifts.

DIALOGUE 121

Rule #37: Mix your dialogue to a consistent level.
Rule #38: Get rid of unnecessary dialogue elements and pauses. Just because it's there doesn't mean it should stay there.

Rule #39: Exercise your authority to change and alter words. Just because they're there doesn't mean they should stay as they are.
Rule #40: Beware of breathing.
Rule #41: Smooth out dialogue by adding continuous sound.

GRAPHICS AND TITLES 133

Rule #42: Whatever you do, use any font other than the default font.
Rule #43: A graphic or title is a visual event and should be treated as such.
Rule #44: Do not fade a title out at the end of a visual cut.
Rule #45: Keep subtitles precise and clean.
Rule #46: If there's a title on screen, viewers will not hear what's being said.

AUDIO MIXING 143

Rule #47: Consider your mix through the proverbial telescope.
Rule #48: Think of mixing as adjusting relative levels.
Rule #49: Use the secret weapon of compression to control levels.
Rule #50: Shape your sound by knowing and using EQ.

COLOR CORRECTION AND GRADING 161

Rule #51: Know the different levels of color tools and what they do.
Rule #52: Know the general techniques of color correction and grading that will have the greatest effect on your project.
Rule #53: Use color grading to adjust attention magnets.

EDITING PROCESS 175

Rule #54: Channel your inner Henry Ford.
Rule #55: Organize your work project. Especially if you're not an organized person.
Rule #56: Never label anything "New."
Rule #57: Organize content on separate and consistent tracks in your timeline.
Rule #58: Adapt your organization to the particular project.
Rule #59: Actively build your bag of editorial tricks.
Rule #60: Duplicate your sequence or project file regularly.

Rule #61: Allow time to polish at the very end.
Rule #62: Set a deadline.
Rule #63: Use whatever pieces of equipment work with your style. Yes, you can use a mouse.

MINDSET — 191

Rule #64: Trust your initial reactions.
Rule #65: Embrace limitations. That's where creativity flourishes.
Rule #66: Take responsibility for details.
Rule #67: Know when to stop tweaking.
Rule #68: Invest yourself and be willing to release yourself at any moment.
Rule #69: If viewers see, hear, or understand something other than what you intend, THEY ARE RIGHT.
Rule #70: The Process is often the Point.
Rule #71: Make your tools invisible by knowing them inside and out.
Rule #72: Adapt or die, because tools and processes change.
Rule #73: Engage with other editors.
Rule #74: Pursue excellence even when it seems like nobody cares.

BEYOND THE BETTER BUTTON — 207

ACKNOWLEDGEMENTS — 211

GLOSSARY — 213

RESOURCES — 219

ABOUT THE AUTHOR — 220

EDIT BETTER

INTRODUCTION

WHY THIS BOOK?

The world it changes, my friend. Yep, sure does. Specifically, the state of the editing of moving pictures is so far removed from its beginnings over a century ago as to be almost unrecognizable.

For the longest time, motion picture editing was a closed-off pursuit reserved for an elite few. Film editors were only hired by movie studios because the studios were the only entities with the infrastructure to edit moving pictures, or to even shoot them at all. It was an exclusive club, and breaking in took years. Once you were in, it took even more years to be allowed to begin learning how to actually shape a scene… instead of just playing babysitter to shelves full of tiny little rolls of film workprint.

Clearly, content creators no longer require a soundstage complex to shoot a movie, or multiple rooms full of equipment to edit it.

EDIT BETTER

These days anyone can shoot video, edit it, and upload it to the Internet using just their cell phone. No exclusive club necessary.[1]

Here's the catch: just because the tools are available doesn't mean that anybody who picks them up will create killer results, any more than placing yours truly in the cockpit of an F-18 makes me a fighter pilot. I assure you, that outcome would not be good.

I'm reminded of a game called Othello that my siblings and I used to play when we were kids. The game consisted of reversible black and white discs and a green playing board laid out in a grid. A slogan on the side of the box informed us that the game required, "A minute to learn, a lifetime to master." I remember wondering, "Who in their right mind would want to spend a lifetime mastering a game like this?" (I've never been one for strategy games.) Even so, the phrase stuck in my mind, and I've found it quite applicable to editing.

You can indeed learn the basics of video editing in mere minutes - swap things around, cut, trim, put music underneath it and upload it to the Internet to your adoring public. It seems like a really easy thing to do. And it certainly can be.

But what people eventually realize is that editing is a complex, multi-layered process that does indeed take a lifetime to master.

As we move along that path of mastery, the more we are confronted by the gazillion different ways to edit any one project, and the process of making those choices often becomes intensely personal. And anything that's personal can get people worked up into a frenzy faster than the immediate seizure of happiness experienced by my dog Saint when you ask him if he'd like to go out for a walk.

---

1 *For an extension of this idea and a peek into my crystal ball, check out* **RULE #72** (Adapt or die, because tools and processes change).

INTRODUCTION

> Me: Hey Furry Butt.
> Saint's ears instantly perk up.
> Me: Wanna go for a walk?
> Saint: BARRRURRUHH!! ARRR!! ARRRR!!!!

Many people inwardly bristle at anyone with the hubris to say, "Here's how to edit **BETTER**," because that idea can easily come across more along the lines of "Your choices aren't good enough" or "You must obeyyy, obedient sheep, obeyyy." Neither being popular concepts in our culture these days.

People then respond with righteous indignation, "I will make my own choices because it's a personal thing and I am going to be me and I'm going to create my own editorial reality and who R U to tell me how to make my own personal choices you stupid big obnoxious judgmental person you stop judging me stupid judger I shall now post sarcastic yet contextless updates about you on social media."

No need for all that, folks, I promise.

I'm not here to stomp on your personal choices. Rather, I'm here to help you consider specific strategies and tactics that will enable you to edit the way you want to… in an even more powerful and effective way.

WHO ARE YOU?

In other words, who is this book for?

It's for anyone who knows editing is not a cakewalk. It goes far beyond "trim the beginning, trim the end" and that's it.

Maybe you're an advanced hobbyist, or maybe editing is something that people hire you to do part-time, or maybe you're a multi-hyphenate type who does everything including the editing. Maybe you're a full-time assistant editor itching to make the jump to full editor.

If you're already an experienced, full-time editor, chances are you already know many of the ideas in this book.[2] But you and I both know that one new idea can make all the difference to your project when applied in the right way. I know of editors with Oscars and Emmys on their bookshelves who *still* have the desire to continuously learn. That's what got them to that award-winning place to begin with.

Who is this book *not* for?

People content to remain Beginners. If you're happy with chopping the beginning and the end of a video clip, putting a title on it and dumping it on the Internet, and that's all you need, then fantastic. That's totally cool. And you probably won't benefit from this book.

It is also not for people who think they know everything there is to know about editing. I certainly don't. But if you do, best to move on, oh omniscient one. Nothing to learn here.

I would submit, though, that if we're not growing, we're dying. If our knowledge is not expanding, it's contracting.

Personally, I'm all about growth. And I'm guessing if you're still reading this, you are too.

---

2   *And to my fellow professionals and artistic peers, many of whom are equally qualified to write this book: if you have additions, clarifications, or bones to pick, your thoughts are welcome at Book@ThePowerEdit.com.*

INTRODUCTION

WHO AM I?

I've been pursuing learning and excellence in communication my entire life. Literally.

My dad tells me that the very moment I was born, I immediately began looking around the room, looking and looking, taking everything in. Curious Jeff, right out of the gate.

I was born in Australia to American parents who moved our family back to the United States before my thick little Australian accent stuck.[3] So I grew up in the Midwest US, mainly South Dakota and Iowa, and showed an early talent for music.

At the age of four, I began piano lessons. I continued through high school where I competed in various music contests, performed a Mozart piano concerto with a regional symphony, and at the end of my senior year gave a Very Serious Performance of Heavy-Duty Classical Works. Rachmaninoff, Chopin, those guys, knowing all along that I would go absolutely nuts if I were to pursue a career as a concert pianist.

Meantime in my junior high years, some family friends gave me a little Casio keyboard, the kind you could buy for $59.99 at Radio Shack. I thought it was the best thing ever and began experimenting with basic multi-track recording, MIDI sequencing, and lots of music arranging and composing.

Then one day in 9th grade, my art teacher suggested that I do a video project. I fell in love with the process, even though I was the only person in my high school who cared about video at all.

---

3   *I used to mourn the loss of my accent, which is well known to make one more attractive to The Ladies. Even my wife admits that her checklist of desirable qualities in a husband included some sort of non-American accent. The silver lining: growing up with what most would refer to as a "neutral Midwestern accent" has helped me to land a decent number of well-paid voice-over jobs throughout my time in Los Angeles. Eh, who needs an accent anyway.*

Of course, my entire high school had 200 students in it, and I graduated in a class of 35 people. It made sense that I was the only person who cared to walk around with a VHS camcorder on my shoulder and learn about editing on a linear, cuts-only editing system. (Hey, who needs timecode when you have control track?)[4]

After two years of college, double majoring in Bible studies and music composition, I transferred to film school out in Los Angeles. I promptly ran out of money and had to drop out of school. Thankfully, I'd been working my tail off and had impressed my professors. The head of the film department gave me a phone number that led to my first job in television.

That first job started as an unpaid internship. My boss asked if I knew the Avid, and I said no. He said that if I wanted to learn, I could show up at night and hang out with the assistant editors. I worked Friday and Sunday nights for six months for free. Years later I found out that one of the most impressive things I did was to continue to show up for six months. To me, it was a no-brainer. As far as I was concerned, they had already hired me and I just wasn't getting paid. Yet.

Having put in my late-night dues digitizing countless boxes of Betacam tapes, I was the obvious choice the next time a paid position opened for a full-time assistant editor. A couple years later, I was promoted to full editor, and I've been editing television in Los Angeles ever since.

At this point, the entities for which I've edited include ABC, NBC, FOX, Universal, Disney, ESPN, MTV, The Discovery Channel and too many more to list here.

Along the way, I have been building businesses like ThePowerEdit.com that help people learn how to communicate more clearly and

---

4 *For any pieces of editing jargon that you might want explained further, check out the Glossary at the end of the book.*

INTRODUCTION

powerfully through video editing. We've had our materials spread all around the world to over thirty different countries, and that's just counting the ones we've heard about.

So, while I have been building my career as a professional editor, I also have a strong desire to help and encourage other editors.

Hence this book.

ASSUMPTIONS… AND YOUR EDITING

One thing I don't want to do is make assumptions about you, the reader. I've made that mistake too many times.

There was one time in particular where I really stuck my foot in my mouth through thoughtless assumptions. I was on an editor's online forum, and someone asked advice for his editing reel. People on the forum began commenting about what should and shouldn't be on your reel, giving the impression that they all had one and updated it regularly.

I of course had the *brilliant* idea of saying that it had been years since I've updated my demo reel, and in my experience the only people who have to rely on a demo reel don't have a strong enough credit list or professional network to get jobs by referral.

With that statement, I managed to insult almost everyone on that forum *and* present myself as an insensitive clod at the same time.

Not my finest moment.

One person responded and said, "Uhh… for those of us not in your position, we actually do need to show prospective employers our editing reels. It may not be that way in Los Angeles, but that's just the way it is out here."

Whoops.

In light of that, I don't want to assume you're in my position or that you even want to be in my position (though you may already be there). For every person out there who dreams of making a living from editing or pursuing some version of the Hollywood dream, there are plenty of others who simply want to create their own projects on their own time.

Here's what I will assume, though: I assume that you love (or at least enjoy) the process of editing, and you want to do it **BETTER**. And I am assuming that you're open to learning. If that's the case, you and I very much have those things in common.

In light of that, I would like to take this opportunity to encourage you.

There was a time early in my career when I was working on a FOX show alongside some experienced fellow editors. One of them, Charlie, was (and to this day still is) one of the most accomplished editors I have ever worked with. He had already put together some segments of the show, and as I watched his work my heart sank. I thought, "Good grief, how on earth will my work ever measure up to *that*?"

At some point I told one of my producers something like, "Man, Charlie's work is so good that I feel like a hack by comparison."

The next day, the executive producer of the show strode into my edit bay.

"I heard you said a really crappy thing," he said sternly.

"What's that?" I asked a bit nervously.

"That you feel like a hack compared to Charlie," he replied. Then he looked me in the eye and said, "Don't you ever say that about yourself. I don't hire hacks, and you do really good work."

INTRODUCTION

That was a pivotal point in my career. Sometimes it takes external validation to give yourself permission to believe you really are good at this.

That process continues. Just as external validation has been a huge encouragement to me throughout my career, I'd bet good money that it's a good thing in your world too, and I'd like to offer some up to you.

Because from where I sit, the sheer fact that you're reading this tells me that you are open to learning. And those of us who actively learn how to communicate more powerfully through editing often find that **our work is already more powerful than we may have given ourselves permission to believe**.

I'll bet you're already pretty good at this editing thing.

So consider that idea, be encouraged, and let's dive in.

THE TELESCOPE AND THE MICROSCOPE

"Would you tell me, please, which way I ought to go from here?"
"That depends a good deal on where you want to get to," said the Cat.
"I don't much care where," said Alice.
"Then it doesn't matter which way you go," said the Cat.
– *Alice In Wonderland, Lewis Carroll*

"If you don't know where you're going, you'll end up someplace else."
– *Yogi Berra*

Editing is at its core communication. Powerful communication functions within a grand scale of intent, meaning, and impact. This scale might be compared to examining the enormity of the night sky through a powerful telescope, the big idea in Part 1 of **EDIT BETTER**.

Editing then performs its actual function of communication by way of thousands of tiny choices and details, nitty-gritty topics that might be compared to examining an object of interest under a microscope, the big idea in Part 2 of **EDIT BETTER.**
I personally believe that you can't fully, regularly succeed in editing unless you have at least a foundational command of both the

telescope and the microscope.

Note the above word "regularly" – it's a big deal. There's a lot about editing that can be picked up by experimentation. Sometimes people edit a piece by sheer instinct, they capture lightning in a bottle, and the audience is blown away by the piece. The editor then attempts to recreate that effect on the audience with the next piece, and it doesn't happen. Why not? Well, there are a million possible reasons. One of them almost assuredly being:

The editor who cuts sheerly by instinct usually doesn't know why the cut does or doesn't work. And it's fiendishly difficult to recreate an effect on an audience that you don't know how you achieved in the first place.

So, towards the aim of nailing the impact of your edit every time, let me offer an additional metaphor.

TACTICS VERSUS STRATEGIES

Imagine you're in a war. You're commanding a platoon of soldiers, and your orders are to capture the hill up ahead. To successfully do that, you'll need to consider ideas in two categories: your strategies and your tactics.

Tactics tend to be immediate, boots-on-the-ground specific things that you do; in this case, specific ways to defeat the enemy and take control of the hill. Would you and your soldiers hide and pick the enemy off one by one with sniper fire? Create a diversion and launch rocket-propelled grenades at them? Those are specific tactics one might use.

Strategies then refer to the bigger picture and are often attached to the question "why?" Why do we need to do this? Why do we need to take this particular hill instead of that other hill over there? Why

THE TELESCOPE AND THE MICROSCOPE

are we in this war at all? What will winning the war accomplish?

In the editorial and communication realm, this book speaks to both tactics (the microscope) and strategies (the telescope) while leaning heavily on editorial tactics. Because frankly, that's what so many people have told me they want, to learn tactical details of editorial practices that seem so difficult to find otherwise.

Here's the thing:

The best editorial tactics in the world are useless without the right editorial strategies.

For example, it does you no good to pull out the microscope and build the world's best opening montage for a scene that should not be in the sequence in the first place.

So in order for us to most effectively get into the details later in this book, let's trek up to the observatory and step up to the telescope.

PART 1
EDITING THROUGH THE TELESCOPE

This part of the book consists of two sub-sections that discuss:

1. The three main hats that need to be worn by the editor, and

2. The core rules of editorial planning.

Once we have those ideas in place, we'll have the groundwork laid to pull out the editorial microscope.

For the record, this stuff is primarily theoretical. If you're dying to get into the nuts-and-bolts practical stuff, move along to Part 2…

…but ignore the Telescope at your own editorial peril.

THE THREE HATS OF AN EDITOR

As with many crafts, there's far more to powerful, effective editing than just juggling clips in your timeline. I tend to speak of three main hats that the editor wears: Technician, The Creative, and Psychologist.

HAT #1 - TECHNICIAN

Think construction worker hard hat. This is the foundational one. To perform the function of editing, you have to know how to use the tools of your editing system, just as a carpenter has to know how to drive nails by swinging a hammer.

This is the hat most people focus on, and the hat that most often pops up when you search for "how to edit video" on YouTube or such – all those videos telling you "these are the buttons, and here's how to push them."

The Guy In The Print Shop

Ever since the invention of picture editing, stereotypes have long been flung about on the perception of editors as "mere technicians."

Imagine placing an order at your local quick print shop for 1,000 4x6 postcards to be printed with full frame bleed on 5x7 pieces of card stock. The print shop guy takes your file, loads the paper, hits the Print button, and uses a giant paper cutter to remove all the extra stuff around the edges. No brains necessary, just whack off the extra stuff with a paper cutter.

Now let's face it – the technical skills needed by that guy at the print shop do not require a mechanical genius. People not familiar with the craft of editing tend to think of it in the same way, as a purely mechanical, not particularly exalted craft.

Were we to more accurately compare editing to the function of that guy in the print shop, the actual role of editing would go far beyond loading paper in a machine, hitting Print, and chopping the extra stuff.

The guy in the print shop would potentially have been responsible for the graphic design of that postcard. He might have written or rewritten part or all of the text on it. He might have participated in detailed discussions with 14 levels of decision makers about the overall goal of the postcard, why it should exist at all, who will be making use of the postcard, and been responsible for building it as a postcard, changing it into a billboard along the highway, then changing it back into a postcard with text only, then with color pictures, and then text *and* color pictures, etc.

And only then might the editor have some involvement hitting Print and whacking off the edges. Maybe.

THE THREE HATS OF AN EDITOR

So the person unfamiliar with what we as editors do might say something like, "Oh, you just cut out the bad parts, right?" While that's true, a better version might be, "We start with lots of separate elements of the [movie/show/video], keep the good parts, get rid of the bad parts, and combine everything in the right way to end up with the finished piece."

The Editor's Role... Then and Now

However, ask different people in the film or TV industry what editors do, and you'll get an interesting range of responses from:

"Editors are WRITERS, they CREATE the story from nothing!"

to:

"Editors are mostly button pushers."

Each statement is at times both true and false, and both are grossly lacking in context.

Wanna insult a professional editor? Call him or her a button pusher, then get ready to dodge flying objects.

Truth is, virtually anyone who edits anything today will do so by pushing buttons on some sort of digital device, and the well-balanced editor needs to know how to wear that hat of button-pushing Technician. But to limit the role of editing to just pushing buttons throws out all of the creative and psychological process that takes place.

Now here's a further element to add to the conversation – there's a certain perception in the editing world that editors who cut feature films are operating on a higher plane of consciousness than editors who have to "lower themselves" to edit television or random video projects.

The grass is always greener on the other side of the fence, my friends, and this includes editorial grass. Editors laboring on low-budget corporate videos dream of cutting primetime television content. TV editors often dream of cutting scripted dramatic television, instead of everything else they have to actually cut. TV editors who cut scripted content often find themselves creatively stifled and underpaid, and they dream of cutting movies. And the elite few who actually do cut movies for anything other than minimum wage have to constantly tap dance around their occasional creative exercises to pacify 29 layers of decision-makers and are meanwhile terrified that they won't be offered another movie to cut.

There's a good reason for all of that.

When motion picture editing was first invented, it didn't have buttons to push – it had scissors, a grease pencil, and splicing tape. And later, pedals to stomp, and a device oddly reminiscent of 18th century French folk: the workprint-chopping guillotine. Physically assembling film workprint – while time-consuming and somewhat annoying – didn't require a lot of training. The assistant film editors often ended up being the ones to do the physical cutting and splicing.

Just like the guy in the print shop chopping off the edges of the postcards. No deep thinking required.

Film editors, from the very beginning, found the most difficult part in deciding **what parts of the film to use and why**. All along, film editors have had to understand and assemble scenes and story in their head while keeping all the important people happy, and that's where years of experience and the deep thinking came into play.

Along come the 1950's and this new-fangled thing called video. Getting video to work required rooms full of crazy, complicated equipment along with an entire team of mad scientist engineers to operate it.

THE THREE HATS OF AN EDITOR

Those guys had to be **real** button pushers, and not just anybody could do it. Instead of going home and saying hello to their wife or their dog, they went home and said hello to their pet oscilloscope.

On top of that, video had technical limitations in how it was assembled (and later inserted). Where film has *always* been non-linear – you chose different sections of workprint and connect them together in whatever order you chose – video for most of its early life was linear. You had to electronically copy down one section of video at a time, in the order that it would ultimately live on the master tape.

If you wanted to change one shot at the beginning, you either had to degrade your edit master by making a copy of it, or you had to Redo The Whole Freaking Thing.

Insert wailing and gnashing of teeth here.

As a result, for many years, video editors were indeed primarily button pushers, because running the machines that made video work required complicated, specialized knowledge.

The creative work of editing was often left to people other than the video editor. TV producers knew that in order to make use of the precious, limited, and **EXPEN$IVE** time using those million dollar rooms full of video gear, they had to have their act together. They had to have a script planned out literally to the second, and the editor helped run the machines that brought that script to life.

This has changed. Big time.

Instead of video editors overseeing an entire machine room of gear and calculating timecodes in their heads, the gear has largely shrunk down into tower or even laptop computers. And software now does all the number crunching, rendering of all your effects, and managing and accessing your media, all that sort of thing.

Producers no longer have to know exactly what they expect the end result to be, and they rely on good editors to realize their visions by going far beyond pushing buttons on complicated machines.

All this to say: because of the technologically simple film medium, film editors have *always* had to be creative storytellers. Because of the initially technologically complex video medium, video editors *used* to be glorified button pushers. But as video technology has progressed, so has the role of video editors, to where professional video editors are now required to be creative storytellers every bit as much as film editors. The genres, budgets, and prestige may differ, but the overall function is now ever increasingly similar.

Back to the idea of Hat #1, The Technician.

This book speaks in only limited ways about Technician-related ideas, which tend to vary wildly depending on your software or tools. We'll let the rest of the world blather on about the best way to pull a greenscreen shot in [insert your current editing program here]. Don't get me wrong, if you've shot greenscreen elements, you definitely want to know how to make them work well. But the most seamlessly composited greenscreen shot doesn't mean much if it doesn't serve a greater purpose.

Which brings us to:

HAT #2 – THE CREATIVE

Imagine yourself wearing a funky French beret, waving your hand, and saying things like "I am an arrrteeeste." This hat requires you as editor to be a creative artist and communicator. You have to figure out what's the best way to combine all the elements into a seamless piece.

This is the thing that's easiest to think that you've got down. It's

THE THREE HATS OF AN EDITOR

the thing that's most likely to tick people off when you speak of it, because so much of the world considers creativity to be intensely personal. "How DARE you tell me how to edit, blah blah blah…"

It's also the thing that's easiest to write off and say, "Aww, well I guess I'm just not creative." Especially in the times when you see examples of creativity that verge on the seemingly miraculous. "How did she come up with that?" audiences ask in amazement. "That sequence is flawless!"

If you've ever said to yourself, "I'm not creative," stop it.

Seriously, stop saying that.

That attitude, my friend, is a travesty that doesn't even deserve to exist in your head.

Replace that horrible idea IMMEDIATELY by beginning to telling yourself instead, "The more I learn, the more creative I become." Your subconscious might argue with you for a while, but keep repeating that sentence, replacing the bad idea with a constructive one. Eventually your subconscious will start to believe what you tell it.[5]

Because I am here to tell you: "flawless" and "creative" results are achievable by anyone who diligently pursues them. They might take a while to get there, but they absolutely are achievable. And these results usually arrive in two ways:

1. Knowing the rules and when to break them. One of my favorite quotes on this subject comes from Pablo Picasso, who advised we

---

5   *For the clinical and medical back-up on how and why this works, read the updated version of* Psycho-Cybernetics *by Dr. Maxwell Maltz, edited by Dan Kennedy. While the title might make it sound like it's pitching a new religion or something (which it's not), it's an astoundingly powerful look into self-image and performance at the very highest levels. Absolute must read.*

"Learn the rules like a pro, so you can break them like an artist." You'll find lots of those rules in Part 2 of this book.

2. Combining existing elements in ways one might not expect. Very few things are ever brand new, never before seen. Achieving "creative" results often comes from throwing something against the wall to see if it sticks. Put shots together that you otherwise wouldn't. Drop in a cue of music that you wouldn't expect – that death metal rock cue might be the exact vibe to go with the shot of the little old lady crossing the street. Then again, maybe not. But give it a shot, who knows?

While people may debate the definition and origin of personal creativity, here's one thing I can say with confidence:

Editorial "creativity" is a skill that can absolutely be practiced and developed by anyone who desires to do so.

It's an essential hat that must be worn by any editor who desires to communicate powerfully through editing.

HAT #3 - PSYCHOLOGIST

This, the third editorial hat, is arguably the most difficult one to wear well. Anyone can learn to push buttons. Anyone can learn to apply and combine ideas in unexpected, "creative" ways. But both the Technician and Creative hats get thrown to the side if they don't work in concert with the Psychologist hat.

You, the Psychologist Editor, must understand the minds of all the people involved with the project at hand. If you don't, the chances of your project succeeding are slim. Here are the three areas that require the Psychologist's understanding: Your boss, your audience, and yourself.

THE THREE HATS OF AN EDITOR

> You as Psychologist must understand your boss.

Most editors who edit for pay do so in service of others, be they producers, the director, the client, or even your friend who's asked you to help out. Your role as editor will not succeed if you don't know what your boss wants and how to deliver that.

If your boss does know what he or she wants, and you know you can deliver that, then BANG. You're in business, and life is good.

Sometimes your boss literally does not know what he or she wants, and it's up to us as editors to play Mind Reader. That's when things can get challenging. Sometimes just frustrating, occasionally outright infuriating.

Some people love that challenge, and others don't. Personally, in my life and career, I specifically gravitate towards people who know what they want and avoid working with those who don't. Life has enough challenges without adding needless extras.

Whether you answer to a specific person or not, your piece will always have a boss in a larger sense:

> You as Psychologist must understand your audience.

I cannot overemphasize how huge a deal this is.

We as editors are communicators. Communication requires a sender (us) and a receiver (the audience). If the sender does not send the communication in a way the receiver connects with, communication FAILS.

If we do not know who our audience is and what they want, our projects will miss their intended marks and end up far from what they could otherwise have been… if they don't outright fail.

I'll be discussing this idea of Audience further both in the Editorial Planning section that's coming up, and in **RULE #69** (**If viewers see, hear, or understand something other than what you intend, THEY ARE RIGHT**).

In the meantime, know that Audience is *huge*.

And lastly:

> You as Psychologist need to understand your own mind.

I kid you not: the more in tune you are with yourself, your strengths, weaknesses, and the ways you interact with storytelling and the world, the more likely you are to end up participating in – or flat-out creating – some amazing projects.

The last part of this book deals with ideas that focus on editorial mindset. These are often the ideas that can only otherwise be learned by screwing up and making mistakes.

Oh, crap. Mistakes. Those are always Bad, right?

Heck no.

I'm actually a huge fan of them. And not because of some masochistic, pain-loving thing either. They're usually not fun, but they're almost always great teachers for those who are willing to learn. Even better, when I'm making a lot of mistakes, chances are I'm making even more really *good* choices.

Make mistakes, learn from them, and do everything in your power to keep from repeating the same ones.

That's what the mindset part of this book will help with… as we all journey towards being more finely tuned Editor Psychologists.

THE THREE HATS OF AN EDITOR

There you have it – the three primary hats that the Editor wears: Technician, The Creative, and Psychologist, with the Psychologist understanding the Boss, the Audience, and the Self.

The next ideas throw those three hats right into the middle of the ring as we continue to peer through the Editorial Telescope.

THE IMPORTANCE OF EDITORIAL PLANNING

Say you were a carpenter, and you had the best, most expensive, advanced hammer that money could buy… I mean, this hammer is the most amazing, high-tech tool ever built, it's incredible. Does the fact that you have this amazing hammer mean you automatically know how to build a house? Of course not. And it's the same thing with editing.

To achieve powerful editing, possession of the tools isn't enough.

Taking that idea further: say you have the World's Most Amazing Hammer, and you have honed your skills such that you can use that hammer to drive a nail straighter than anyone else around. Does that mean that you know how to build a house? Nope.

To edit pieces that create strong, emotional responses in their audiences, possession of the tools isn't enough, and knowing how to use the tools isn't enough either.

When it comes to really communicating powerfully through editing, the most important factors are not related to tools at all. The fact is, you can have the biggest budget in Hollywood and the fanciest, shiniest tools of the trade, and that won't be enough if you don't get some foundational factors in place first.

So what are the foundational factors?

These factors are mental choices… made before and during the edit. These choices are equally important to a video seen by only a handful of family and friends, and primetime network television show seen by millions.

In short, these choices are all about Planning.

Here's something to consider:

THE MOST POWERFUL IDEA IN THE WORLD IS ONLY POWERFUL WHEN DIRECTED TO THE RIGHT PEOPLE… THROUGH THE RIGHT CHANNELS… IN THE RIGHT WAY.

Think about it. If you want to build a house you wouldn't have a bunch of stuff delivered to a vacant lot and start building. No, first you hire an architect, then the architect draws up the blueprints, and only then does the process move forward.

But as anyone who's ever worked with an architect knows, huge questions have to be answered *before* you start laying out any sort of floor plan.

An architect would ask questions like…

- What style of house will this be?
- Who will live there? What do they expect out of a house?
- What are the constraints for the house in time and money?

THE IMPORTANCE OF EDITORIAL PLANNING

Only *after* answering these sorts of questions do we consider how to lay out the floorplans.

In the same way – bringing it back to video editing – the decisions you make *before* you begin are mission critical.

And if, like the carpenter, you happen to have the World's Most Incredible Hammer, all the better. But you start with the planning, you start with the blueprints.

And that's the key – no matter what project you're doing, no matter whether it has a huge budget or no budget, the planning is the number one foundational choice that will give you the greatest chance of creating those powerful emotional effects in your audience that we're all looking for.

So at this point you might be thinking, "Great, planning is important. That sounds kind of boring and generic. What does that actually mean?"

Glad you asked.

EDITORIAL PLANNING: THE RULES

Editorial planning hinges on five main words. I tried to be fancy and have them all start with the same letter, because alliteration is cute and memorable. Alas, I only made it to four. The words are:

> Outcome
> Message
> Market
> Media
> Method

But really, the acronym here is even better. Remember the ideas like this – when you put the rules of editorial planning into place for your projects, your edits will be grounded and at peace with themselves, like those people in yoga class folded all pretzel-like, going "OMMMM, OMMMM."

Booyah. Cute and memorable, yes?

Here's the main idea: First decide *what you want to happen* as a result of the audience experiencing your project (Desired Outcome). Then decide *what you want to say* (Message), then *who you want to say it to* (Market or Audience), then *the channels through which you communicate* (Media), and last, *how you say it* (Method).

While a case can be made for some of these ideas to be addressed in a different order than listed above, they generally work best when applied in the above order.

Now before we go into detail on these ideas, there's an element of planning that we should address first – the timing of planning.

The big idea here is: **Plan early. Then plan later too.**

Editorial planning is most powerful when done *before any shooting*. However, once the shooting or content origination is done, the planning rules still apply to your editing whether you've planned before the shoot or not.

Even the biggest budgeted, best planned projects require an editor who knows how to use these rules. The more they're integrated with planning before shooting, the better. But even *after* shooting, they're still critical to putting together the elements that you, the editor, are shaping.

Time to break it down. Here we go.

THE IMPORTANCE OF EDITORIAL PLANNING

RULE #1 | DETERMINE YOUR DESIRED OUTCOME.

Were both Sir Isaac Newton and Stephen Covey still around, I would buy them both a drink.

Newton's 3rd Law of Motion states that for every action, there is an equal and opposite reaction.

Covey, in his hugely popular book *The 7 Habits of Highly Effective People*[6] encouraged his readers to "Begin with the end in mind."

I say put the two ideas together: begin with the end in mind… by first deciding what you want your audience's final reaction to be.

In other words, determine your Desired Outcome. Ask yourself, **"What do I want my audience to experience, know, or do after they experience my project?"** Do you want them to be entertained? Inspired? Become enraged and storm out the door waving picket signs or calling their legislators? Convinced or persuaded of a new idea?

This is ground zero of all editorial planning.

Achieving your Desired Outcome then requires the application of the following **strategic** planning rules, plus the judicious use of the right **tactical** rules later in this book.

Thing is, few people ever talk about this idea of "what do we want to happen as a result of this project?" It's usually either obvious, taken for granted, or not considered at all. And in the real world, Desired Outcome usually ends up a mixed bag of action to be taken, ideas to address, etc.

---

6   *If you haven't already done so, I highly recommend you read or listen to it. There's a reason it's sold over 15 million copies and been translated into 38 languages. It's just that powerful.*

But think about it – if your Desired Outcome changes from "I want people to think I'm the greatest editor ever, look at me edit" to "I want people who watch this piece to change the way they interact with the world"… well, then you have to start asking things like:

- "What ideas do audience members currently hold to, and how would I want that to be different?"
- "Who are these audience members, and why do they think the way they do?"
- "How should I shape my project to communicate in a way that is most likely to be favorably accepted by the audience?"
- And all sorts of other big-picture questions like these.

So instead of just glossing over or completely ignoring this foundational concept of Desired Outcome, make sure you give it the consideration it deserves.

Because it affects literally everything still to come in this book, and in your edit.

RULE #2 | DETERMINE YOUR MESSAGE.

Having begun with your Desired Outcome in mind, it's time to actually say something. Or at least decide what you want to say via your message.

Message comes in lots of different forms.

It could be a theme addressing love, anger, revenge, relationships, or good vs. evil.

It could be a specific message, like a piece of news on TV saying "the governor met with people affected by the flood" or "last night huge movie stars came to the premiere of their latest movie, here's what they had to say."

THE IMPORTANCE OF EDITORIAL PLANNING

Your message could be a general idea, like a family video showing that "we had a great time on our vacation to Hawaii."

Every project you do has a message of some sort – the question is, **are you going to actively shape it or not?**

The most powerful projects, and certainly the pieces you will do by use of these rules of Editorial Planning, actively say something by design. The creator of the piece actively chooses to communicate the message of his or her choice.

Now you can act as if you have no idea what a message is – just throw something together and put it out there. That's asking for your project to fall flat on its face. That's a virtual guarantee that most people will *not care* about your piece at all, because it either has nothing to say, or it says it in a confusing way. Pieces that fall flat or don't connect with their audiences often have a lack of focus in their message. Again, every piece *will* have a message of some sort – it's up to us to shape it.

And now, a warning: some people rely on toys and gadgets to substitute for an actual Message. For the sake of your projects and your audience, do NOT fall into the trap of "I shot with cool toys" or "I have cool special effects in editing" to take place of *actually having something to say*.

When I was in film school, everyone was really impressed when a project looked good enough like it was shot on film instead of video. Sometimes the person who did the project would say "Yeah, we shot on Super 16" – or even more impressive, "Yep, our DP's got the hookups to shoot on 35." And everyone in film school would go "whoaaa, that's amazing," and we'd all be jealous and wish we could do projects on 16 or 35. But that didn't mean the project actually said anything. It certainly didn't mean that the project was any good.

It doesn't matter whether you shoot on the fuzziest cellphone camera or the most tricked out hotshot cinema camera – or whether you use a piece of free editing software or a room full of the most expensive, powerful editing machinery available…

…message comes first.

I certainly didn't start out knowing the importance of message. When I was in 9th grade, my art teacher said "Jeff, I think you should do a video." I figured sure, why not, so what did I do? I was gonna make a video, so I figured I should get some video equipment. I went to the school office, borrowed a VHS camera and a tripod, set it up in an empty classroom, and… I sat there scratching my head. I had no idea what to do next.

I went back to my art teacher and asked her about what my video project should actually say. She said she was going to give a presentation to the school board on the school's technology, so maybe I should do a video about the school's computers that she could show to the board. That sounded fine to me.

I put together an outline and starting shooting interviews with teachers. I was especially excited to shoot my very first insert shot – the teacher was demonstrating replacing a RAM chip in a computer, and I shot a separate close-up that showed everything in detail. I thought that was the best thing ever, just like the close-ups they do in the movies.

After I shot everything, I took a day off from school. I wasn't even old enough to drive yet, so my mom drove me to the state-funded edit suite an hour away. I shuttled through stacks of tape on VHS editing decks the size and weight of an armored tank, and I had an absolute blast putting that project together.

THE IMPORTANCE OF EDITORIAL PLANNING

Well, I showed the video to my art teacher the next day, and I was so enthralled with my first project that I didn't notice she didn't say much of anything. I'd had a fantastic time putting together a long, rambling, disjointed piece that was so boring, you could actually feel your brain cells dying.

I believe there are a total of 5 people who have seen that video in its entirety. The school board never saw it – somehow my art teacher never got around to asking me to show it there. Go figure.

Moral of the story: my message was *way* off focus. Sure it was about the school's computers, but I hadn't really zeroed in on what I wanted to say. The result was a piece that was unbelievably boring, and it's sat in a box gathering dust ever since high school. Who knew that project would find its eventual calling in being a cautionary tale?

Some people have told me, "Jeff, why are you being so hard on yourself? You were 14 years old!" And that's certainly true, there's little point in expecting a beginner to execute like a seasoned pro.

But decades later, that temptation still pops up every once in a while. We've all experienced that seductive pull of relying on smoke and mirrors or secondary things to pull our projects along instead of driving it through clearly defined Message.

To achieve powerful communication, we must plan our Message. Don't let it happen by accident, decide what you want to say on purpose.

EDIT BETTER

RULE #3 | DETERMINE YOUR MARKET. WHO IS YOUR AUDIENCE?

Once you know your Message, you need to know who that message is going to. Why?

Because different audiences want different things, and they want to be spoken to differently.

And, to get a little ahead of ourselves, guess what? Different audiences respond differently to different Media… your great-grandmother is probably not going to watch videos on her cell phone. If she even has a cell phone.

So before you start shooting and editing online videos for a market who may not know what your media outlet even is, never mind how to use it, it's better to consider more questions about your audience in the first place. To do that, let's talk about the way Markets have evolved since the beginning of this whole editing thing.

Deep Thoughts on the History of Markets

For anyone who thinks that the following is getting overly philosophical or theoretical, stay with me. Unlike high school calculus, the following ideas do have application to your life.[7]

When modern editing first existed, it functioned mainly for movies shot on physical film, produced by a small number of movie studios. Technology progressed to include video, which was used mainly by television stations. There were a bunch of TV stations producing local news, but the main television shows were produced by a handful of television networks.

---

[7] *To those select few who have managed to apply the plotting of cotangent curves to the non-academic world, I salute you.*

THE IMPORTANCE OF EDITORIAL PLANNING

Compared to today, there were very few movies being produced and only a handful of TV channels on the air, controlled by a very small group of people.

What did this mean?

It meant that everyone watched everything literally because it was there.

If you and your friends wanted to watch a movie, there were only a few movies out in the theaters, so you watched whatever was playing. Television shows came on at a specific time in the week, and *everyone adjusted their schedules* to watch their favorite shows that aired on only a handful of TV stations.

And video editing was a very technical, specialized skill that required access to movie studios, television stations, or production companies with very expensive equipment. Not available to the general public.

Fast forward to today: content creation is no longer the domain of the exclusive few.

The technology used in content creation and video editing has progressed to where it is now available literally to anyone with a computer. Heck, you can even edit on your cell phone if you want to.

A small number of movie studios still dominate the large-scale movie production world, but independent filmmakers have been creating their own movies for a long time now. Television is no longer the domain of major networks, and it's become a torrent of content, hundreds and hundreds of channels that viewers can choose, record specific programs, and watch them whenever they want.

What does this mean?

It means that instead of yesterday where everyone watched everything, today no one watches everything.

People today are much more interested in "what specifically do I like to watch whenever I feel like it?"

The "Big General Markets That Everyone Fits Into" have become the "Many Small Niche Markets That People Choose For Themselves." These days people have access to every little niche they could ever want, and it doesn't matter if it's music, TV, movies, or whatever, they are very, very picky.

The Big General Market is DEAD.

Today, it is more important than ever before to choose a specific market that will be open to your message.

Who are they? Get specific!

Do *not* say, "Everyone is my audience!" That doesn't even work for Warner Brothers or Universal Studios anymore. Because they know, and you need to know, the moment you say "everyone is my audience," you are setting yourself up to play to everyone in general… but no one in specific.

The result: everybody will feel like you're not talking to them, so they'll be bored. Or just not care. Both of which are bad.

How then to describe our niche market? You can do it in a few words, or an entire multi-faceted breakdown. Thankfully, there's an easy starting point – if you had only one question to ask about clarifying who your niche market is, it would be this:

THE IMPORTANCE OF EDITORIAL PLANNING

What do members of the ideal audience have in common?

Here are some potential commonalities:

- Who they are (demographics): Gender, age, racial background or language.
- What they do for a living.
- What they enjoy doing (hobbies): Fishing, gardening, home improvement, extreme sports.
- How they think, believe, or view the world (psychographics): culture based on location/region, religion (or lack thereof), politics.

Why, you ask, is it important to think about these things?

Because different audiences want different things. And it's our responsibility to read their minds (as the Psychologist Editor) and do everything in our power to give them what they want.

This applies to large, sweeping generalities: men, by and large, watch different TV shows, movies, and video content than women. Audiences over the age of 50 want different content than audiences in their 20's.

It applies to more specific scenarios: a 35-year-old Korean businesswoman will resonate with a video differently than will a 35-year-old British businesswoman. A teenager in Oregon will consume different content than a teenager in Texas.

But then take something like a psychographic commonality, like politics, and you might end up with the teenager in Vermont valuing the same content as the Korean businesswoman.

Does Market Ever Come Before Message?

Now earlier I said that most times the order of strategic editorial planning goes like this:

>Outcome
>Message
>Market
>Media
>Method

That's generally the most effective order for things. Of course, for every rule in this book, there is an exception. Here's one:

Many times content creators will start with an idea, then say "who out there should be interested in this?" That happens a lot with inventors and entrepreneurs too – *"I've got this Amazing Idea, now who should it be marketed to?"*

This idea is what most people do. The screenwriter writes an amazing, complicated script… that never finds its audience. An entrepreneur starts a business… that never finds its customers.

Some very smart people have found great success by first saying, "Who is my market, and what message do they want to hear?" Once you figure that out, it's much easier to give it to them. You start out with a starving market who wants what you're about to give them, as opposed to creating a work that then searches aimlessly for a home.

So what comes first, the Message or the Market? As is often the case, it depends on the project.

Broad strokes: If you're looking for your project to have commercial

THE IMPORTANCE OF EDITORIAL PLANNING

viability – as in, have people willing to pay money to experience it – market is *hugely* important.

If you're creating your project mainly for yourself, then create away however you see fit.

But the truth is, "Message or Market first?" is not the right question to ask. Both affect the other, as does all your strategic planning.

Which brings us to the next strategic planning rule.

RULE #4 | DETERMINE YOUR MEDIA.

Ask yourself, "What channels of delivery will my project use?"

A lot of people start with this first. I certainly did in high school when my art teacher said "hey, you should do a video" and I said "uhhh, okay."

Not the best plan.

Now let's be realistic – I'm not gonna get all uptight and say "you must NEVER begin with the medium." It's okay to know what your delivery mechanism will be from the very beginning – it's just that if you are serious about creating powerful results with your video editing, your choice of media absolutely must interact with the rest of the strategic planning rules we're talking about.

Earlier I offered this idea for your consideration:

THE MOST POWERFUL IDEA IN THE WORLD IS ONLY POWERFUL WHEN DIRECTED TO THE RIGHT PEOPLE... THROUGH THE RIGHT CHANNELS... IN THE RIGHT WAY.

This statement doesn't just talk about powerful ideas. It talks about how all the elements interact with each other – and because of that, you can replace "idea" with other things to modify the statement like this:

THE MOST POWERFUL MEDIUM IN THE WORLD IS ONLY POWERFUL WHEN THE RIGHT MESSAGE… IS DIRECTED TO THE RIGHT PEOPLE… IN THE RIGHT WAY.

How will your audience see and hear your piece?

Certainly, we're talking here primarily about video editing. It's a pretty safe bet that your audience will experience your project on some sort of display that shows moving pictures. But that's an idea that's easy to take for granted – there are all sorts of ways audiences experience creative works other than watching a screen:

- Still images – physical photographs, online images, posters on a wall or a street corner, billboard along the road
- Just sound – podcasts, traditional radio or satellite services
- Just words – newspapers, magazines, graffiti on the wall
- In person – artists speaking, singing, or dancing in front of one person, or a whole crowd.

But like I said, we're talking about video editing here, so let's stick to outlets that have moving video.

Bear in mind, asking the question "what channels will I use to spread my project?" brings on a multi-part answer. Saying "I am editing a feature film for theatrical release" means that you're editing a project that is intended to be shown in movie theaters. But that says nothing about the companies and distribution routes that will be employed in the process.

THE IMPORTANCE OF EDITORIAL PLANNING

That conversation of addressing all the distribution entities for your projects is beyond the scope of this book. For our purposes here, let's just consider the question of viewing devices – because they bring issues into play that you may not have considered.

Viewing Devices

Just as the world has changed with the idea of markets and who consumes what content, viewing devices have evolved as well.

When moving pictures first started out, most people saw them on a big movie screen. Then people saw early television shows on small TV screens that went from black and white, to color, then bigger screens, and bigger and bigger until these days some of these TVs actually *feel* like a movie screen they're so big.

But now the extra element is computers – and as technology progresses, the size of computers gets smaller and smaller until you're holding your own personal viewing screen in your hand. So ask yourself, what devices are your videos most likely to be seen on?

Will it be computers, tablets, phones, or television sets? How about large format or theatrical outlets, with your project shot up on a movie screen or even taking up the side of a building?

Why, you might ask, does it matter what devices will be used to view your projects? It matters because the devices will affect how you put your projects together.

(Screen) Size Matters.

Here's a general rule: **The smaller the screen size of your delivery medium, the more close-up your shots need to be.**

If you upload a video that you know will be seen mostly by people watching on their phone, then you can't show big wide shots of the countryside with lots of details in it and expect the viewer to see those details. You have to choose more medium and close shots to make sure that the audience sees what you want them to see.

Now if your video is going to be shown on a movie screen or some huge television, you have more latitude in shot selection. Use those sweeping establishing shots. And at the same time, you better keep in mind that the hilarious shot of someone's face filling the entire screen might be amazing if you're watching it on your phone… but showing that same shot on a two-story-tall screen could be downright terrifying.

But that's just one of the really cool things about having a big screen to work with… you can literally have an actor stand in the middle of a wide shot, and not do a thing except raise their eyebrow, and it communicates everything you need to know. Whereas if you use that same shot on a tiny video shown online, nine out of ten people will completely miss the point because they don't see all that beautiful detail.

Other variations to consider:

- Image and sound quality – are there technical requirements or limitations to keep in mind?

- Low vs High. Will your project have highly compressed video shown on mini screen, or uncompressed video projected against a

THE IMPORTANCE OF EDITORIAL PLANNING

building? Audio that sounds like it's playing through a tin can, or audio that's so detailed it sounds like you're sitting in the middle of the recording studio?

• Multi-channel? 3-D video and surround sound? Or just one stream of picture and one little channel of audio? No judgments here… there's a reason and a place for every scenario.

You don't have to have all the answers for this at the beginning. Sometimes there's no way to know the answers until the project's finished. So in that case, a good question to ask is:

"What is the highest quality version of this that will actually be needed?"

If the answer is "I'm shooting and editing on my cellphone and uploading it to Facebook," then you don't have much to worry about. If the answer is "the project will air on broadcast television," you'll have a bunch more issues that you'll be dealing with along the way. Most of them are beyond the scope of this conversation here, though many will be addressed in Part 2 of this book.

Reality check for those who are asking, "I thought this book was about editing. When do we actually talk about that?"

We are. Granted, keeping the screen size and technical requirements of your project in mind won't actually get the editing done, but they absolutely affect the way the editing actually happens.

And now that we've considered what we want to see happen (Outcome), what we're saying (Message), who we're saying it to (Market), and the channels through which our project passes (Media), it's time to talk about how to do it (Method).

RULE #5: DETERMINE YOUR METHOD, THE DRIVING IDEA OR UNIFYING CONCEPT BEHIND YOUR PROJECT.

After the preceding ground work, everything starts to come together. And here's the irony: choosing the Method – sometimes referred to as a Treatment – often is a very quick process. Sometimes it feels like it takes forever, though, because we get all caught up in the questions that we should already have answered with the other M's. But when all those questions of

- What is my Desired Outcome?
- What is my Message?
- Who or what is my Market?
- What are my Media?

are answered, often the idea of Method (How do I communicate the Message) just falls into place. For the times that it doesn't, choosing your method can be helped along by asking questions like the ones that follow. First, a reminder – like most of the strategic editorial planning rules, considering your method is most effective before the project is shot. Many times, though, we as editors are brought on to a project and are expected to bring our ideas for editorial method to bear on projects that are already completely done shooting.

In my editing career, more often than not the people who hire me have a general idea of what they want, but they may not know exactly how that would work in the edit. In those cases, they rely on me to bring my own editorial ideas to the table. Sometimes my instructions are literally, "Hey, we went out and shot this stuff, here's who it's for, now do something cool with it."

So, whether you're considering your method before or after the shoot, that choosing process can be helped along by asking the following questions.

THE IMPORTANCE OF EDITORIAL PLANNING

Do I have any available elements that might shape the project?

• Are there elements that you personally own that could be contributed to the project? I, for example, own sound effects libraries and royalty-free stock footage that I regularly use, depending on the project.

• Is there anything you could go out and shoot or acquire on your own? I've had jobs where I needed extra images that I didn't have access to at the time, so I went out and shot them with my personal camera. I knew exactly what the piece needed, my extra elements worked out perfectly, and I got brownie points from my producers for taking the initiative to make things happen.[8] This can also be something as simple as recording a couple extra lines of background dialogue with a microphone to explain things or fill in some editorial gaps.

• Are there elements available online? Any image or sound you can imagine, it's probably available on the Internet somewhere. Some elements are very obviously copyrighted and shouldn't be used. Other images are so common, it's impossible to say who owns them.

For the record, I'm very much a supporter of respecting the intellectual rights of content creators, just as I expect others to respect my rights. Some projects are highly restrictive on what elements are allowed to be used, usually broadcast or theatrical projects where people could get sued if you use the wrong stuff. Or maybe your crazy-good Youtube mashup video cut to that amazing song… that's copyrighted, and Youtube yanks it. Sigh.

And other projects don't really matter at all what you use.

---

8   You think the other editors on that show were going out and gathering extra elements for their pieces? Heck no – that wasn't their job. Hmph. In the meantime, that extra effort to make the piece better made me stand out from the rest of the editorial crowd, and it can do the same for you.

What style does your Market expect?

This is a big deal. If you as the content creator/shaper are going to give your audience what it wants, you need to know what they expect.

Oh, and that's another reason that it's important to know who your market actually is… first. Because a style that works for one audience may not work for another.

What does your audience expect for:

- Mood? Tense, happy, relaxed, energetic?
- Music? Old standard songs, movie scores, electronica?
- Pacing? Fast, middle of the road, relaxed?

I once edited a pilot for the CMT channel – originally, the pilot was quickly paced, very tongue-in-cheek, like animated shows with the constant one-liners. We sent it to the network, and they said, "We love it! Now change it for our audience – slow it waaaaay down."

Now does everyone who watches CMT here in the United States love NASCAR racing, country music, and lazily sitting on your porch with a case of beer? No, that's too general a stereotype to expect all a network's viewers to fit. But that's the image that the network cultivates, and that's the laid-back stylistic treatment that my producers and I were expected to ultimately deliver.

Then there was a pilot for MTV, the media outlet who since the 1980's has very visibly pushed the editorial pace of television faster and faster, and even popularized the use of jump cuts in TV and video editing – something previously horrifying and inconceivable to most people. The music, pacing, and energy of the MTV pilot was everything you'd expect from an MTV show – go go go go. It was exhausting to edit, to tell you the truth.

THE IMPORTANCE OF EDITORIAL PLANNING

So one way to find your piece's method or treatment is to consider what your audience expects, then give it to them. Now, the opposite idea:

What might your Market NOT expect?

Let's face it – people may think they know what they want. Often, they'll be just as happy with something they're not expecting. Just ask the wife or girlfriend whose expectations for Valentine's Day are instead blown away by something different but even more thoughtful than the flowers and candy she was expecting.

Audiences *love* to be legitimately surprised. Be careful attempting this though, because audiences have come a long way from the early days where a shot of a train approaching the camera sent people stampeding out of movie theaters in terror.[9] Modern audiences are hardened cynics, and they are hard to surprise. Do it right, and you will reap huge rewards.

Yet another reason to make full use of your Psychologist Hat, yes?

Unexpected Funny… or Not.

Unexpected elements weigh heavily in comedy. It's one of the main reasons we laugh – expecting one thing and experiencing the opposite. Or better yet, watching someone *else* experience the opposite. We'll be talking more about this later, especially when discussing **RULE #17 (Play peek-a-boo with your audience by use of The Reveal).**

---

9   Many attribute this story of extreme public reaction to the 50-second-long, single-shot film called "Arrival of a Train at La Ciotat" released by the Lumiere Brothers in 1896. Others label it an urban legend.

How might your project's method set up a scenario that then switches? This could end up being funny, or not funny at all.

Poor Louis Armstrong. His song "What A Wonderful World" is a regular victim of treatments that purposely play opposite the song's contented, peaceful lyrics. "And Ah think to myselllf, what a wonderful worrrrld…" is just as likely to play under all sorts of horrible things – scenes of murder, violence, nuclear holocaust – as it is to play under anything uplifting, happy, or wholesome.

A note to those desiring to be smug, cynical, or hiply ironic, please don't put nuclear bombs over "What A Wonderful World." It's no longer hip or ironic, it's just overdone.

Method via Production Values

Often your method will be a reflection of – or will be shaped by – your production values, the general quality and overall scale of the project. This usually exists between two extremes:

- Homemade or Low Budget – there's a reason people use this look. Home video-styled pieces communicate a certain unpolished, real feel that can be very effective for the right projects.

Or:

- Projects with Large Budgets. An hour of reality television being shot for a million dollars an episode means you can do some pretty flashy things. And a feature film being shot for $200M means you can fly around the downtown skyscrapers with actors dangling from helicopters. You can also hire a raft of graphics companies to modify the scenes so the modern day characters are simultaneously performing as cavemen dangling from pterodactyls in a Stone Age forest.

THE IMPORTANCE OF EDITORIAL PLANNING

Of course, this kind of stuff is generally only possible when there's actual money involved.

And for every editor who gets the pleasure of cutting a project with a large budget and significant production values, there are thousands who are stuck somewhere else.

Keep in mind, though, that no matter the production values, it is equally possible to convey a strong, compelling message whether your project was shot in your garage or in front of the Taj Mahal.

Homages

Are there existing examples that you might want to emulate? A very wise man once wrote that there is "nothing new under the sun." It's rare to come up with something that's completely different from absolutely everything else.

How might you shape your editorial method to "walk in the footsteps" of previous works? If you know a formula that works, why not use it and add your own twist?

On the flip side, is there a very obvious example of something in your project that will remind people of other works in ways you don't want? Sometimes homages work really well, and sometimes they, well, don't. The more obvious the similarities, the riskier the homage tends to be.

Here's an example – an eminently quotable and homage-worthy line comes from the 1983 movie *Scarface* where the drug kingpin played by Al Pacino sees an army of henchmen coming to lay siege to his mansion. Grabbing the nearest machine gun he roars, "So you wanna play rough? Okay, SAY HELLO TO MY LITTLE FRIEND!!"

He opens fire, blasting open the double doors of his upper story lair onto a balcony that overlooks the front lobby and fountain of his palatial estate. He proceeds to send bodies flying with his machine gun, all the while screaming in a cocaine-fueled rage.

The body count is high, the scope of the scene is jaw dropping, and it's sorely tempting to make some sort of reference to it, whether in one's own projects or just throwing out the "SAY HELLO TO MY LITTLE FRIEND!!" line in random conversation.

Say you want to include an homage to the *Scarface* "LITTLE FRIEND!!" scene in your project. Of course, this would probably involve having roles in the project that go beyond just editing.

Do you want to do a direct comparison? As in, bloodshed, carnage, and mass mayhem? If you do, ya better do it up big. Because a scene between two characters squeezing off a few shots at each other from subcompact pistols just doesn't measure up.

Now a deranged, gangster-movie-loving Third World dictator referencing his "LITTLE FRIEND!!" as he waves his finger over a red button that sets off a nuclear holocaust… that would work as a direct comparison with its own unique twist.

Here's something else that would work:

Two young boys hide behind the bushes, shooting a water gun at the kindly looking grandmother sitting on her front porch in her favorite rocking chair. As the water hits her, she sighs and reaches for her knitting bag, which contains a book of crossword puzzles, a few skeins of yarn, and a ring of keys. She presses a button on a remote control on her key ring.

Another squirt from their little water pistol hits the elderly woman, and the boys snicker in glee, not noticing the sudden rumble of the air compressor from the back yard of the lady's house, triggered by pressing the button on her remote control. Grandma smiles sweetly at

THE IMPORTANCE OF EDITORIAL PLANNING

the boys behind the bushes as she reaches under her rocking chair and picks up a wand for an industrial strength power washer. "Say hello to my little friend," she quips, letting loose a cannon-blast of water that sends the horrified pair of boys screaming down the street.

That would work too, whether you've ever seen *Scarface* or not. Which brings up another point about homages: will your audience actually recognize them? Will the homage stand by itself if they don't?

If the homage falls flat without audience knowledge of what you're referencing, and you're not absolutely sure that most of your audience does know it, then don't do it.

You might feel all cool adding that shot of a baby carriage rolling down the front steps of a building – "It's art, man, it's an homage to the Odessa Steps scene from *Battleship Potemkin*!" – but if that shot doesn't make sense when viewed by a non-Russian-cinema-familiar audience[10]… lose it, Eisenstein.

Where do you now stand?

So here they are, the Rules of Strategic Editorial Planning, through which we view editing through the proverbial telescope:

RULE #1: **Determine your Desired Outcome** – what you want your audience to experience, know, or do after they experience your project.

RULE #2: **Determine your Message** – what you actually want to say through your project.

---

10   *Let it never be said that I'm making light of the Odessa Steps sequence. It's one of those truly seminal pieces of editorial art that deserves every accolade and homage it has prompted over the years. What? You've never searched "battleship potemkin odessa steps" on YouTube? Do it. Now. Seriously.*

RULE #3: **Determine your Market** – who **specifically** is your audience?

RULE #4: **Determine your Media** – what channels of delivery will your project use?

RULE #5: **Determine your Method** – the driving idea or unifying concept behind your project.

Here's the next question you have to ask – **do I now have a blueprint for my project? Do I have a decent idea of how to move forward?** The answer could be yes or no.

If the answer is yes, then carry on – there's much to consider in the rest of the book here.

If the answer is no, consider spending some time reviewing the above rules.

Because all the ideas in the world about editorial structure, edit points, music editing, color correction, and mindset are pointless if you don't have at least some idea of where you want to go.

And now… let's step away from the telescope, knowing that we can always come back if needed (which often is a good idea anyway).

It's time to pull out the microscope and get into the details.

"Learn the rules like a pro, so you can break them like an artist."
-*Pablo Picasso*

"There is no one way to edit."[11]

-*Jeff Bartsch*

---

11 One of the really sweet things about writing your own book: putting your own quote right next to one from Picasso. I could get used to this.

PART 2
EDITING THROUGH THE MICROSCOPE

What follows is the nitty gritty, the obsessive-compulsive side of editing.

Many of these following ideas and rules are never discussed because people either assume that the editor knows them, don't care if the editor knows them or not, or don't want to potentially insult the editor by questioning things on such a detailed level.

Other rules to follow are indeed discussed in other venues, but hardly ever in conjunction with editing. Some might wonder about the inclusion of ideas more commonly raised in business development, acting classes, and behavioral psychology – I say we sell ourselves short if we limit the wide-ranging subject of editing as communication to only editing itself.

Time to reiterate:

Every single rule in this book has an exception. Sometimes a whole bunch of exceptions.

This book is not about telling you what to do. It's about setting up a jumping-off point for you to do your editing the way you want to.

EDITORIAL STRUCTURE

One could argue that editorial structure is a big-picture idea that should be included in the previous section with the rules of editorial planning. And that's initially where it lived... until it became clear that the rules of editorial planning supercede anything in this section.

Now that we've gotten more of a feeling for what the project actually *is* in the big scheme of things, we can put the following tactics into play.

RULE #6 | UNDERSTAND THE PIECE BEFORE YOU BEGIN EDITING.

I once heard a story about some students in an editing class, and one of them was an old-school film editor who had joined the class to learn how to use the new software. The professor said, "Here are the dailies we're working with for this scene. You have a certain amount of time, now go."

So the college students jumped on their computers and started grabbing parts of scenes and throwing them into their timeline. While they were trying this and that, the older editor watched down every single piece of footage, taking notes on a yellow notepad. After he finished he consulted his notes, chose a handful of source clips, assembled them in his timeline, and that was his scene.

When the time was up, the students all played back their scenes. Some of them worked and some of them didn't. Most used more edits than were necessary. But even though the old-school editor only had a handful of edit points in the entire scene, each one cut like butter. The scene played as smooth as glass. And the college kids realized, "Wow, this guy really knows what he's doing."

The reason the film editor was able to do that – other than the fact that he'd been doing it for forty years – was because he had trained himself to get the whole idea in his head, fully understand the piece, and then build it out.

As we discussed earlier in the Editorial Hats section: when editing was first invented, film editors had to put their scenes together in their head first. While the physical organizing and splicing pieces of film was not technically involved, it was still a lot of work to take all these pieces of workprint, separate the source reels, assemble the desired sections, and then file away the extra pieces. Putting a scene together was a big deal.

And when video editing was first invented, the refrigerator-sized machines required involved, highly technical processes to copy sections of video to a compiled edit master. And it all had to be done linearly, one shot after another, from beginning to end. And if everything worked except that one shot at the beginning, you had to reassemble the whole thing. So a television producer had to know exactly what she wanted before walking into the edit bay, because it was so expensive.

EDITORIAL STRUCTURE

If a producer walked into an old-school linear edit bay and said as so many do these days, "Let's just try this and see what happens," he would be up a creek without a paddle. But now that technology has progressed, there is room for infinite experimenting. We now have more opportunity to try different solutions to editorial scenarios, but technology has also released us from the need to know what we want to do before we start.

This is both good and bad.

The speed and relative simplicity of modern editing technology doesn't really save much time, because **the time the technology could save is often wasted by messing around trying to figure out what you want to do in the first place.**

Now to be sure, experimentation is a critical part of the creative editorial process. Experimentation is good. Blind experimentation with no idea of the desired end product? Ehhh… that tends to be less than ideal.

So while the rest of the world jumps right in, fiddling with their cut trying this and experimenting with that, invest the initial time to really mentally absorb the materials on your editorial plate.

Because you will achieve the best results all that much sooner[12] if you know where you're going from the beginning.

---

12 If you have unlimited time to explore and polish, fantastic. Have fun and enjoy the process. If you are being paid to edit, the project almost always has a limited amount of time and money for you to do your thing. In which case, quickly getting to the place you want to be is good. Ideally, it will give you the time to make the piece everything you want it to be.

EDIT BETTER

RULE #7 | **WHEN IN DOUBT, START WITH WHAT YOU KNOW TO BE IMPORTANT.**

I've often heard editors say, "I have a gazillion pieces to work with. How do I start?"

Here's how. Imagine a very large, empty jar, and your job is to completely fill it up. You place a number of large rocks in the jar.

One could say the jar is now full, yes? No, not really.

You then add a bucket full of medium sized stones to the jar, filling it just underneath the lip of the jar.

Is the jar full now? Not yet.

You add a bucket of sand to the jar, which filters down through the large rocks and smaller stones until the level reaches the lip of the jar.

Surely the jar must be full now, right? No it's not, and stop calling me Shirley.[13]

You pour a bucket of water into the mix of rocks, stones, and sand, and it fills up the jar until the sandy water is just about to spill over the top of the jar.

Is the jar full now? Why yes, it's full. Absolutely nothing else will fit in it. Everything is there, including all those big rocks that you put in from the very beginning.

Back to "I have a gazillion pieces to work with. How do I start?"

---

13   *Movie quote. Homage to a movie that I'm reasonably certain the bulk of people who read this book will recognize.*

EDITORIAL STRUCTURE

Start with the big rocks. Begin with the core elements of the project that you know will be in there, and fill in the smaller connecting pieces later.

RULE #8 | PUT YOUR STRUCTURE INTO VISUAL FORM.

The longer and more complex your piece, the more involved the overall structure will be. Your piece might break down into scenes, or sections, or thirty-second pods. The more complicated things get, the more you will benefit from having a specific visual reference point of the overall structure.

Honestly, this can be something as simple as scribbling a list of the sections on a piece of paper. Better yet, assign each section to its own 4x6 index card so they are moveable and you can rearrange them as needed. You can even get colored cards and arrange them that way too.

The first time I experienced this was when I was editing a reality show for ABC. As often happens, the plans for the episodes had changed after shooting, and I was getting confused which scenes were going in which episodes and in which order. Out of sheer desperation I grabbed a stack of sticky notes, wrote down the name of each scene on its own note, and started arranging them on the desk in front of me.

Lo and behold, a miracle! I now had a visual representation in front of me that I could show my story producer, and we could say, "What if we change this? What if we swap these two scenes?" All we had to do was move a post-it from one place to another, it made sense, and my brain stopped hurting.

Recently, I was working on another television series which as of this writing is in its fifth season. It has ten episodes per season, and each is broken down into scenes that are two minutes or less. For each 44-minute episode there are between 30 and 40 scenes, many of which last only thirty seconds.

As you might imagine, organizing 30 scenes per episode takes some doing.

The story producers covered an entire wall of the office with index cards. They had ten columns, one per episode, and each column had about thirty cards positioned from the ceiling all the way down to the floor. When story lines started changing, index cards were shifted and swapped, and the producers and editors were all able to stay on the same storytelling page.

The longer your piece, the more involved your structure will be, and the more you will benefit from a visual reference.

RULE #9	FIND THE BACKBONE OF YOUR PIECE AND HANG EVERYTHING ON IT.

Framework holds things together. So does a solid foundation.

Ever built a skyscraper? Nope, me neither. I do know a few things about the process though – the construction of every towering structure begins by digging a great big hole in the ground. Once you've laid the foundation, you begin building the superstructure, the supporting framework of the building. That framework allows you to start adding other sections with steel or cement. Then you add floors and walls, and only after you have all that done do you start painting the hallways and laying carpet (the things people will notice).

Towards the goal of establishing the editorial structure of your project: if you've already started with the "big rocks" of what you know to be important **RULE #7**, and you've done the work of arranging a complex project into visual form **RULE #8**, you may already be off and running with your edit.

EDITORIAL STRUCTURE

Having said that, here's an additional tactical angle: timelines of different projects are built around different elements.

If you're editing a documentary, your piece might be driven by on-camera interview sound bites. If so, you will often build your sequence most effectively by getting all those talking head bites gathered in the correct order in your timeline. Then start thinking about the different non-interview sound-ups and B-roll that will fill in the gaps.

If you're editing a scripted piece, your sequence will probably be driven by dialogue. Begin by laying in the master shots of your scenes, then your reverse shots and closeups. Unless of course you've already planned out the shot sequence that you want, and that you're going to start on that one amazing closeup, then the reaction shot of character #2, then pop out to the wide master shot. Or something like that.

If you're editing a music video, then you already have your editorial backbone – the song itself. Are there any elements that you know need to hit certain parts of your music track? Those are the "big rocks" of your piece that you can drop into the jar first. Add the other elements around them.

Choosing the wrong element for your editorial backbone can be hugely frustrating. I recently heard a woman speaking of how she had slides from a Powerpoint presentation in her editing program, and she was trying to record voiceover for each slide. Yet somehow she couldn't talk fast enough to fit all that voiceover into the 4 seconds of each slide!

Yep, this actually happened. Obviously, the lady had next to no experience editing anything.

But her frustration was very real. And let's face it, we've all had times where we felt like we're painted into an editorial corner like the lady with the Powerpoint slides. Sometimes that's actually true, and **other times we just don't know what we don't know.** In this case, the lady had been looking at the wrong element as her backbone – her piece wasn't driven by picture, it was driven by voiceover. All she had to do was record the voiceover, then adjust the picture to fit.

> **RULE #10** | **PUT YOUR MAIN PIECES IN PLACE BEFORE ADDING ANYTHING FANCY.**

If the main pieces change, your fancy filler work often won't fit anymore. If the architect decides to remove an entire floor of the skyscraper, no one will see the fancy little lamps the interior decorator spent hours arranging on that floor. It will all be gone.

Get the big rocks in place before you add the stones, sand, and water.

I learned this the hard way. Early on in my editing career, I often spent time shifting through footage to build a fancy montage, only to learn the entire scene was being removed. It didn't matter that I'd spent an hour cutting a slick little 15-second montage – that hour had been wasted.

The same goes for adding effects or finishing work. Generally, wait to add those until you're either sure the scene won't change, or you're at a point where you need to add finishing touches.

Here's one of the times worth giving the exception to the rule. Two exceptions, actually:

- Sometimes you have to completely build out a project before you show it to someone. Experienced executives usually know enough to not get all bent out of shape if the piece is not color corrected, or if the audio isn't 100% mixed, but the fact is, **not all executives or project overseers have a sense of imagination.** Though it might

EDITORIAL STRUCTURE

sound a bit judgmental (Stop judging them stupid judger!!), I assure you it's not a moral pronouncement; it's a morally neutral, flat-out fact. If the person(s) that you need to make happy don't "get it" unless everything is completely present and polished, do everything in your power to show them the piece only when it has reached that place.

- If you're working for someone for the first time, and they don't yet have a sense of trust for what you bring to the table, often their mind can be set at ease if you do some early polishing for part of the piece. Sometimes it's worth it to make the first minute of the piece look polished, flashy, and/or amazing, just to demonstrate that this is what the final product might look like. But the rest of it you want to keep fairly basic. Get that overall structure in place. Build the proverbial walls and install the windows before you start hanging the curtains.

GENERAL RULES FOR EDITING

This, like all sections of this book, makes no claim to be exhaustive or complete. I fully expect it to evolve with future editions of this book.

In the meantime, here it is in its current state of Awesomeness.

> Cynic: Wow, this guy really thinks he's something, calling this stuff Awesome. Pffft.

Actually yes. I do. I love this stuff. It's the foundation of what I do every day, often completely losing track of time in the process. I hope you feel the same way about your editing.

EDIT BETTER

> **RULE #11** — READ WALTER MURCH'S *IN THE BLINK OF AN EYE* TO UNDERSTAND WHY EDITING WORKS AT ALL.

The edit is a blink.

And by "the edit" I mean the act of changing from one image to another, which is what our eyes do when we blink.

Before I go any further, I want to acknowledge the writings of Walter Murch on this subject. His book, *In the Blink of an Eye,* was a game changer in how I thought about editing and its function, both on the big scale and the small scale. As far as I'm concerned, Murch's book should be required reading for everyone who has even the slightest interest in editing and how it works. Absolutely required reading.

Here's a two-part explanation of why the visual edit works at all:

When we are speaking and come to the end of a thought, we often blink physically. Ever noticed that with people in person or in the pieces you edit? Watch for it, and you'll be surprised at how often it happens. Just by observing people on-camera or in real life, you'll see that our brains process ideas and concepts in phrases and sections.

So in terms of editing, the brain is already open to the idea of changing and switching. That's part 1.

Here's part 2 – our brains process changes of image much like a visual edit. We can observe this by noting our own stream of vision.

Try this right now: you look at thing "A" on your left and then you turn your head to the right to look at thing "B." When your vision shifts from Focal Point A to Focal Point B, do you remember what happened in the middle, that visual information that would otherwise look like a swish pan?

GENERAL RULES FOR EDITING

Try it again. Thing "A," quickly shift your eyes to Thing "B." The swish pan in the middle doesn't register at all. Our brain filters out that unnecessary information, and that's one of the theories of why editing works: switching from shot to shot mimics how the brain operates.

Even something as simple as a cutting or fading to black at the end of a piece is completely familiar to our brains. It's the exact same as eyes open… eyes shut. Cut to black. Boom.

This is only scratching the surface of what Murch discusses throughout *In The Blink of an Eye* – read it.

RULE #12 | ACTIVELY DIRECT THE VIEWER'S ATTENTION.

This idea changed my editorial life. I'm not exaggerating. This is something one of my early mentors told me, and I still think about it multiple times each day:

We as editors are responsible for telling our audiences where to put their attention.

How do we do this? We use our knowledge of attention magnets and physiology to direct the audience's eyes, ears, or mind to different elements of the project at different times.

Attention Magnets and the Sorting Machine

Our brains follow a complex, interrelated set of rules in order to decide where to focus our attention.

Think of your brain as a giant sorting machine that pursues one goal: to make sense of everything. It wants to put everything – and everyone – into categories and boxes and compare what it gets with what it expects.[14]

Your brain hums and sputters inside your head, constantly receiving input events from all your senses, and it has to constantly decide what stuff to pay attention to, and what to ignore. **Frankly, most people's brains have to ignore more things than they can actually pay attention to.**

This is why you can sit in a quiet room, concentrate on a specific task, and be completely unaware of an obnoxious buzz coming from the room's light fixtures. I mean, who in their right mind would actually pay attention to buzzing light fixtures when YouTube has so many life-changing videos of baby pandas to be watched? Come on, now.

This is also why you can witness a multi-vehicle accident and have no memory of things like license plate numbers, clothing of people involved, or even how many people were involved in the first place! No matter that fellow human beings might be injured or maimed… your brain instantly decides that all that extra stuff is completely secondary to cars crashing and almost flipping over right in front of you, which is simultaneously dangerous and amazingly fantastic. *That's* the whole point, says your brain.

This idea of selective attention and your brain's thinning out of sensory input applies directly to editing in the way the audience's attention moves from one thing to another, depending on what grabs its attention.

Or in other words, your **brain moves its attention from one place**

---

14   Non-editorial outcomes of this: stereotypes, prejudice, pigeon-holing, faulty assumptions, you name it. It can get ugly. On the bright side, this process also brings forth hunches, learning from past experiences, and general life lessons.

GENERAL RULES FOR EDITING

to another based on the power of what I call attention magnets. Imagine standing in an art gallery filled with paintings. Here's how your brain sorts what you see:

• In an otherwise blank space containing one single object, our eyes will be drawn to that object.

• If an image contains multiple unrecognizable shapes (say a grouping of straight and curved lines) and one very recognizable shape (the outline of a tree), our eye is drawn to the shape we recognize.

• If a black and white image contains one piece of color, our eyes jump to the color.

• When we see anything resembling a face, the focal point usually ends up being the face's eyes.

• If anything with a face is looking in any obvious direction, the audience's attention will be moved towards the same direction.

Now imagine leaving the gallery of paintings and walking down the hallway to another group of rooms displaying projected video images with accompanying soundtracks. The attention magnets listed above all still apply, but now we have more magnets to add because of the moving video:

• Motion is the great trump card, one of the strongest attention magnets that exist. Our eyes are instantly drawn to motion over almost anything else.

• Motions that are accompanied by sound are more magnetic to attention than motions without accompanying sound.

• Picture trumps sound. Our brains rely more on what we see than what we hear.

EDIT BETTER

We could talk about attention magnets all day, but we'll stop here.

Let's leave the art gallery and sit down at your editing system.

RULE #13 | GUIDE THE VIEWER'S EYE WITH SEQUENTIAL ATTENTION MAGNETS.

Now that we've discussed what attention magnets are, here's the next level: using them sequentially. Here's why this is important:

The viewer's eye constantly roams around the video frame. It's our job to pull it around and make it land where we want it.

How? By using visual attention magnets that pull your audience's eye to a specific place in the frame, creating visual focal points at certain points in time.

Within each sequential shot of your edit, focal points change and move around. This presents both a huge challenge and a huge opportunity for us as editors.

What follows is a secret that explains things that are often otherwise unexplainable:

The most sure way to create a visually smooth edit is to have the outgoing focal point of shot A… be in the same location of the frame as the incoming focal point of shot B.

Let's break that down:

Imagine the frame of our edited piece broken into four quadrants – upper left (Q1), upper right (Q2), lower left (Q3), lower right (Q4).

The viewer's eyes are constantly scanning the picture frame. The viewer's brain is sucking in all that information, sorting and categorizing

GENERAL RULES FOR EDITING

as it always does, and it wants to know what it should pay attention to. The savvy editor chooses shots that contain attention magnets that in effect say to the viewer's brain, "Direct the eyes to this spot right here in Q2, because this is important." Given a powerful enough attention magnet, the brain says "Okay, that looks important – eyes, move to Q2." The eyes dutifully snap to that important spot in Q2.

This all takes place in a fraction of a second. And then the shot changes. The viewer's brain says "alrighty, new shot, better scan the frame to make sure we're only paying attention to the most important stuff."

Where does the brain start? It starts wherever the viewer's eyes happen to be at that instant. If Shot A ends with a visually magnetic focal point in Q2, and the shot changes, the viewer's eyes will be looking at Q2 of Shot B.

If the visually magnetic focal point of Shot B is also in Q2, the viewer's eyes don't have to move. The brain says, "Aha! The most important thing in this Shot B is right here where the eyes were already looking! Just stay right there, eyes, I'm gonna go grab a powdered donut."

This, my friend, is what creates a visually smooth edit. It means your eyes don't have to jump around the frame searching for the next focal point, because they're already in the right place as the next shot arrives.

Now imagine we have the outgoing focal point of Shot A in Q2, and the viewer's brain has decided that Q2 is indeed the place to be looking. Shot A ends, in comes Shot B.

But the focal point at the beginning of Shot B isn't in Q2.

Whoops.

This is what creates a jarring or rough edit.

The viewer's brain says, "Um… Q2 is obviously not the place to be looking. Eyes, let's rescan the frame so we can decide where we're actually supposed to be looking." And the viewer's eyes start roaming around the frame, providing all the information that the brain can organize and decide what's actually worth its precious attention.

After a few nanoseconds the brain says, "Here in Shot B, we say the important place to look is in Q3. Eyes, hang out in Q3." And the eyes snap to Q3 and say "Hey, we want a powdered donut too, dammit."

This process of deciding to move the eyes from Q2 to Q3 happens in mere fractions of a second. But it's a process that interrupts the viewer's brain from fully concentrating on the piece. No matter how subconscious or brief, it's still an interruption.

And mental interruptions are felt as rough edits.

So here's the moral of the story: when you sequence your shots, always ask yourself, "Where is the viewer's eye?" Make sure the eye is not jerked around, but rather smoothly directed from shot to shot by use of actively chosen focal points created by the rules of visual attention magnets.

When you do this you will not believe how much more smoothly your cuts play.

RULE #14 | SHOW WHAT *IS* BY CONTRASTING WITH WHAT IS *NOT.*

Many years ago I was doing my laundry at a laundromat, and a nearby television was blaring away. The overall volume wasn't that loud, but as my loads of laundry progressed, I found my ears getting tired listening to that TV.

GENERAL RULES FOR EDITING

"Why on earth are my ears getting tired listening to a TV set that isn't all that loud?" I wondered, folding my t-shirts and bath towels. Well, I've since learned why. It wasn't that the volume level on the TV was exceptionally high, it's that all the different pieces of sound coming out of the speakers were equally loud. Eventually, the sound became physically difficult to listen to.[15]

Suppose you're at a restaurant, and all the food is sweet. At the end of the meal, they bring out dessert. Surprise, it's sweet. The dish might be your favorite dessert of all time, but since it's surrounded by all this other sweet food, it's just not as good as you remember.

Contrast makes all the difference.

If everything is loud, loudness loses its power. Loudness is most effectively felt in contrast to quietness.

And if every edit is fast, fast editing loses its power. (Plus it takes forever to edit too.)

In editing, if you show a continuous element of something that is either depressing or fast or slow or brightly colored, the power of that element will diminish the more that it's surrounded by things like itself.

To truly emphasize the uniqueness of what *is*, you must provide enough contrast to show what is *not*.

---

15   Audio engineers and musicians refer to it as "ear fatigue." A highly technical entry on that great source of general knowledge, Wikipedia, refers to it as "listener fatigue."

EDIT BETTER

RULE #15 | SEEK SIMPLICITY BY HIGHLIGHTING ONLY WHAT'S IMPORTANT.

As the story goes, early film viewers seeing a shot of a steam train rolling straight toward the camera stampeded out of the theater in terror. By the mid-20th century, audiences had gotten used to things like wide shots, close ups, and tension and danger within visual storytelling. But visual storytelling was still stiff and traditional in many other ways. If a scene began with Man 1 sitting at a desk in his office, and Man 2 knocked on the door, entered, and began a conversation, the editor would show every… single… part… of the action.

> Shot 1: Man 1, wide shot at desk, working.
> Shot 2: The door. Knock, knock.
> Shot 3: Man 1 looks up from desk. "Yes?"
> Shot 4: On door. Man 2, behind door, says "May I come in?"
> Shot 5: Man 1 nods. "Certainly."
> Shot 6: Door opens, Man 2 steps through.
> Shot 7: Master shot of Man 2 walking across the room to the desk.
> Shot 8: On Man 2: "Hello, Fred."
> Shot 9: Man 1: "Hello, Hank."
> Shot 10: Man 2: "May I sit down?"
> Shot 11: Man 1: "Please do."
> Shot 12: Man 2 sits down. "I was thinking about something this morning."
> Shot 13: Man 1: "Yes? What's that?"
> Shot 14: Man 2: "I realized that blah blah blah…"

Good grief. I'm going nuts just writing all that meaningless fluff. Seriously, 14 separate shots for what today would take at most four. Or probably start right at Shot 14. But that's the way it was – everything had to be completely spelled out in excruciating detail.

GENERAL RULES FOR EDITING

Eventually filmmakers pushed the envelope of visual storytelling to where these days they can get by with less explanatory scenework. Television? Well, the more movie-like the show, the more experimental it can usually be. Otherwise much of television is still very much stuck in the clutches of Explain-Everything-In-Ridiculous-Detail-Because-Otherwise-The-Audience-Won't-Get-It executives.[16]

Whatever your project, see how simple you can make it. The more clearly you focus the elements of your project, the more powerful its communication is likely to be.

Just know that it's easy to make something complex – achieving simplicity is surprisingly hard. But it's worth it when you do.

RULE #16 | BE AWARE OF WHAT YOU'RE EXPLAINING AND WHAT YOU'RE NOT.

Yin to the previous rule's yang.

If we don't provide enough information and context, our story is less likely to make sense. There are different schools of thought on this. In the world of film, people love to be obtuse. Some filmmakers are jaw-droppingly good at it and leave the audience with their jaws on the floor.

Other filmmakers who aspire to that level of execution purposely mess with the audience and make them think one thing… and then another… and then, "This is what we explained, but we didn't really mean it. Awww yeah, fooled ya suckers." Insert rounds of

---

16 *This might seem like a cynical, "stop judging them stupid judger" statement. I assure you, it's another morally neutral statement of fact. For more discussion of this, check out* **RULE #69** *(If your viewers see, hear, or understand something other than what you intend,* THEY ARE RIGHT*).*

self-congratulatory patting on the back and thoughts of "I'm so amazing. And so artistic. Yay me."

Here's the thing… there is a fine line between engaging and enraging.

The confused mind says "no."

In the filmmaker's quest for creative storytelling, simplicity, or both, it's easy for movies to take it too far to the point where the audience says, "I don't get it." And when audiences don't understand something, they disengage, and the project loses its desired impact.

This happens constantly in short films. There are a million and one ways for a short to fall, well, short of its makers' aspirations. Aspiring moviemakers – or editors who want to edit movies – often start with short films because they're less expensive than full-blown features. But the thing is, shorts are often more difficult than full-length features because they don't have 90 or more minutes of running time to fully explain and develop storylines.

Short films by their very nature have to constantly say more with less. The idea is usually, "We don't have enough time or money to establish context and build a whole narrative, so we'll just assume the audience will accept this stuff." Sometimes that works, but more often it doesn't.

And that's one of the primary reasons that short films fail – they don't properly establish context, or they leave context so undefined that the audience just doesn't get it.

GENERAL RULES FOR EDITING

Beware the spoon.

Television, on the other hand, is all about spoon-feeding the audience. You can't just show a gal walking into a room with a bunch of friends, saying, "Surprise! Happy birthday!" and show a cake. You have to have a friend say, "Okay, so the birthday gal is about to come in. We'll see what happens." And then you see her walk in, and then you go to an interview bite where she says, "I walked through the door, and you'll never guess what I saw!" Then you cut to in-scene, "Surprise! Happy birthday!" And then back to the birthday gal saying, "I was so surprised!" And then back into the scene where here friends say, "Have some birthday cake!" Back to an interview bite where she reminds everyone, "And they got me a cake!"

Sigh. That, my friend, is too much context.

So here's the challenge: movies tend to give too little information, television often goes to the opposite extreme and gives too much information. Striking a healthy balance of what is explained and what is left to the audience's imagination is really hard, and it takes a lot of practice to consistently get it right.

If you have to lean one way or another, explain more rather than less. Because if you over-explain, the worst that will happen is the audience says "Okay, I get it" or "Ha, I already figured that out, I'm smart." If you under-explain, the audience will say, "Uh, I don't get it… and this piece sucks."

Remember, the confused mind says "no."

RULE #17: PLAY PEEK-A-BOO WITH YOUR AUDIENCE BY USE OF THE REVEAL

Reveals are endlessly fascinating and entertaining to little kids. But kids don't know them as reveals, kids know them as "peek-a-boo."

Mother hiding her face behind her hands while playing with her baby: "Where's baby? Wherrrre's baby?"

Baby smiles in anticipation.

Mother pulls back her hands revealing her face. "Peek-a-boooo, I see youuu!"

Baby squeals in happiness.

Peek-a-boo never, ever gets old. Not even to adults. Of course, when we become adults, we stop calling it peek-a-boo. We give it more grown-up names like "audience engagement" or "unexpected plot twists."

As editors, we need to play peek-a-boo with our audience. Why? Because it sucks them into the piece, and when done well, the audience eats it up like a 1-year-old hoovering a bowl full of orange-colored crackers shaped like goldfish.

This can take place on both a large scale and a small scale… with or without snack food.

Reveals on the small scale

Engaging your audience on the small scale can happen with something as simple as one well-planned shot. Usually the shot starts by showing Thing X, then pans, tilts, or moves to reveal More of Thing X.

GENERAL RULES FOR EDITING

It can be as simple as a shot of your favorite movie actress standing impeccably dressed on the red carpet; the shot begins close-up on her custom shoes and custom pedicure, tilts up to show the evening gown and whatever it does or doesn't cover, and ends up on the star's beaming/pouting face.

Or a single-shot reveal can happen by sticking a camera out the window of your car on a roadtrip, like the roadtrip my wife and I took from Los Angeles to Colorado this summer. Driving through Arizona and Utah, you honestly had no idea when the canyon you're driving through would open up to reveal a huge expanse of desert or some sort of crazy rock formations in the distance. It was kind of nuts.

Now editors might say, "That's all well and good, but I'm not doing the shooting. I just use what other people shoot." You're absolutely right. But we can always be on the lookout for well-composed shots that start in one place and end in another by revealing the new, unexpected, or engaging.

Reveals on the big scale

If your project has a big reveal within a story or character arc, often that will originate with the writer or producer. But not always. Sometimes you have an active role in shaping the overall arc of what the audience knows, what they don't know, and then you can add a turn at the end that changes everything.

Ask yourself: **How can I more firmly establish a beginning context that can later be changed to lead to a reveal on the larger scale?** Because it's those big picture reveals that will more firmly engage your audience in the piece. If major plot twists are not in your control, what *is* in your control? You will always score points with your audience by showing them a new insight.

Again, a word of warning: be careful what you offer to your audience as a plot twist or change of context. Audiences are getting more and more sophisticated. They've seen it all, and they're bored.

Having said that, audiences want to see progression and change, and they love to be genuinely surprised. When the audience is fully engaged, they care more about what you're saying, and your piece will be much stronger.

RULE #18 | BE WILLING TO ENTER A SCENE ALREADY IN PROCESS.

Often when editing a conversation between two characters, the conversation begins with extra stuff that isn't important. Especially with non-scripted shows. Field producers on reality or documentary shoots often have people talk to each other about unimportant things to get into the flow of natural conversation, then switch to the topic they're supposed to talk about. The result: conversation feels more natural than just starting in a way that feels stilted or stiff.

This idea isn't just for non-scripted content. In any editing, ask yourself, "Is this part actually important?" Most often, the unimportant stuff comes at the beginning of a scene or section. See how much you can leave out and have it still work. You'll be amazed at how many times your projects are more clear and concise.

Now for the record, entering a scene late does not necessarily mean cutting short the beginnings of shots, as discussed in upcoming RULE #21 (**Begin a shot just before an action begins, leave when the action ends**). You can do both at the same time. Beginning a scene in mid-process is a separate decision from what visual motion or content takes place at the very beginning of the shot.

If a scene in a diner between two characters begins mid-conversation at a good spot, you still want to make sure the shot doesn't begin

GENERAL RULES FOR EDITING

with Character 1 halfway through turning her head, or Character 2 with his coffee cup halfway to his mouth. In most cases, show the full action, since that's what we're used to seeing in real life.

RULE #19 | CONSIDER EDITING BACKWARDS.

I'm not talking about playing the whole piece in reverse, and I'm not talking about editing through a rear-view mirror.[17]

I once edited a pilot episode of a studio competition show that featured magicians competing against each other in front of a panel of judges. Now the typical way of assembling a show like that is to take the elements of the show from beginning and work forward to the end. My executive producer and I decided to take a different spin on things.

Remember **RULE #10** (**Put your main pieces in place before adding anything fancy**)? With that particular show, the Big Rocks in the Editorial Jar would have *seemed* to be the magic performances, because they truly were the heart of the show. Then you'd cut the judging sections, and the rest of the bits with the host, etc.

But here's the kicker: if you cut the performances first, you might cut the performances to highlight elements that the judges don't mention, and vice versa. It's a recipe for, "Oops, the judges were all talking about this one thing I didn't show. Guess I better recut the performance."

Survey says "ERRRRNN!" Wrong answer.

---

17   Although I actually have used a rearview mirror a few times over the years. Occasionally the editing system that I'm using happens to be positioned such that my back faces the doorway of the edit bay. One day as I was editing away, someone snuck up behind me and yelled "BOO!!" Instead of having a stroke or striking someone with a blunt heavy object, I decided to make a trip to an auto supply store, buy a little rearview mirror, and tape it to my computer monitor. People stopped sneaking up on me. Technology is a beautiful thing.

EDIT BETTER

Edit smarter not harder, people. I am *so* not a fan of needless re-editing. So here's the twist: we do it backwards. **Instead of cutting the big important chunks first, we cut the *results* of the big chunks first.**

We start by cutting the judges' commentary so we know what their most important or insightful points are. That way when Judge #1 says "I loved when you did Thing X," I know to include the performer doing Thing X and to go to a reaction shot of Judge #1 nodding approvingly.

So when you have a project with lots of pieces to go in, start with the biggest, most important pieces, and if applicable, consider building from the results backward. That way you'll know how to best shape the edit so everything you've set up in the beginning pays off in the end, and it won't take a gazillion recuts to get where you want to be.

RULE #20 | BE WILLING TO EXPERIMENT.

Alfred Hitchcock was famous for visualizing and planning every single shot of his movies in advance. He so completely created the movie in his head before shooting that he viewed actors as necessary nuisances, saying things like "I never said all actors are cattle; I said all actors should be treated like cattle."

Very few people in the world are like Alfred Hitchcock, for better or for worse. So for us mere mortals, it helps to experiment. Go in with a plan, but be willing to experiment with things you did not expect.

The power of experimentation has been demonstrated since the earliest days of editing. In the early 1900's a Russian filmmaker named Lev Kuleshov made a short film with a popular Russian actor named Ivan Mosjoukine. The film cut from an expressionless shot of Mosjoukine to a plate of soup, then back to the actor's face, then to a girl in a coffin, then back to the actor's face, and then to

GENERAL RULES FOR EDITING

a woman lying on a couch. When the film was shown to an audience, they raved about the actor's performance - showing hunger when he saw the soup, grief when he saw girl in the coffin, and lust when he saw the woman on the couch.

But it was the exact same shot of the actor each time. The point Kuleshov made was that new meanings can be perceived by the audience depending on what shot follows another. So it behooves us to put together things that we may have not planned.

Suppose you're cutting a montage of a boxer training for a fight. You think you'll only need shots of him hitting the punching bag and wiping sweat away and running laps up and down the stairs. Well, that works, but what if you threw in something you hadn't planned? What if you cut to a closeup of his eyes shifting from one side to the other? It has nothing to do with him training, but the intensity in his eyes could make running up those stairs look a lot harder.

Another thing to try is switching elements around in unplanned ways. One time I was cutting a graphically driven piece, and I had images playing at certain times in various boxes on the screen. I showed it to my supervisor, who was also an editor, and he said, "What about this?" and swapped two clips. At first I thought, "That's going to mess up the way the boxes fly around on the screen!" But then, all of a sudden, they popped in and out in ways I hadn't planned, and it looked really cool. I would never have discovered that look had my boss not switched the shots.

And to take this even further... be willing to experiment even when your director, producer, or client wants to do something that you actively *don't* want to do because you think it's a terrible, horrible idea.[18]

---

[18] *For more on this, see* **RULE #68** (Invest yourself and be willing to release yourself at any moment).

The longer you edit, the more dialed-in you become to people's expectations and what makes them happy. Every once in a while, though, people ask you to do something that you *hate*…

…and… it ends up being really good.

In which case I recommend picking your jaw up off the floor and telling your director or producer, "That was a really good call. I'm really glad you suggested that."

This will help you in multiple ways, trust me.

Be willing to experiment. You never know what might happen.

THE SINGLE EDIT

Here's editing under the microscope in all its nitpicky, obsessive-compulsive glory:

Video runs at 30 frames a second.
(Or 29.97, or 25, or 24, or whatever.)
When I'm choosing the next edit point, I have 30 choices *every single second*. Which one do I choose?

It's a legitimately frustrating question for many, not only because those who ask are in genuine search for an answer, but also because there's no one good answer. And most editors would never even dare to answer the question at all because of the possibility of stepping on somebody's creative shoes, or giving an answer that is incomplete.

Well, screw that. Let's talk about this.

"How do I actually choose the exact frame for the edit point?"

I used to really get myself worked up over this. I mean, there's gotta be a frame that's The Right One. But how do you know what it is? How can you know?! I couldn't… take… the… pressure!! AHHHHH!!!

After a few years of editing professionally, I eventually realized – most times it's a very low-stakes choice. To state it plainly, many times the answer to "which frame do I choose for the edit point?" is:

"It really doesn't matter."

[Cue record scratch and crickets.]

Uhhh… say what?

Yep. Notice the wording: *many times* the exact cut point isn't absolutely critical.

And now, editorial purists – and certain film school students who think their film degree automatically makes them the next Spielberg – will wring their hands and say, "But, but… there's gotta be an exact frame! Walter Murch says he plays down each clip, hitting 'stop' until he hits the exact same frame three times in a row!"

And you'd be right. Walter Murch does that. He's also edited on *Apocalypse Now*, *The Godfather* movies, and is the only man to ever receive two Oscars for Best Editing and Best Sound Editing on the same film (*The English Patient*, 1996). He's a living legend, and he edits cinema that is often widely regarded as Art.

Let's all agree: there are projects that you and I obsess over and treat as Art, and everything else which comprises the vast majority of what we edit.

THE SINGLE EDIT

Most of the pieces we edit are not Art. Most of the edit points in these pieces will not stop working if they happen on Frame 2 instead of Frame 5. Or even Frame 22.

Now let me be clear here:

I am NOT saying that editorial detail doesn't matter.

There's a reason this book contains over 50,000 words, people.

On the contrary, I have built my reputation in Hollywood by being absolutely meticulous with my work – even to the point of sometimes being obsessive – so that the message of the piece communicates as clearly and excellently as is within my power.

Personally, I want *nothing* under my editorial control *ever* to detract from achieving the most effective communication possible. Having said that:

Many edit points work just as well as another, while others benefit from a closer eye to detail.

The difference between the two can be subjective. Knowing the difference between an edit point that matters *more* and an edit point that matters *less* is the mark of a skilled editor.[19]

As with all of this book, the following ideas are far from exhaustive. But they have definitely helped me, and I believe they'll help you too.

---

19   Sometimes the answer to "which is the best edit point" has very little to do with the actual edit point at all and everything to do with the person whose opinion is being offered or imposed. Viva the Psychologist Hat, yes?

EDIT BETTER

RULE #21 | BEGIN A SHOT JUST BEFORE AN ACTION BEGINS, LEAVE WHEN THE ACTION ENDS.

This may seem like a no-brainer, but it's not. How do I know? Because I see editors, beginners and seasoned professionals alike, leaving beginnings incomplete or endings dangling in the wind...

ALL. THE. TIME.

Evidently certain people think, "I want to show The Thing this certain shot has, so I'll make sure it happens... well, at some point in there." The result? The shot begins with nothing happening at all. Then we see whatever we're supposed to see.

Don't do that. Begin the shot either just before The Thing begins, otherwise you have empty space at the beginning for no reason, which feels weird to the viewer.

In most cases, do not begin *while* The Thing is happening. If you cut to a reaction shot that shows someone raising their eyebrow, but the eyebrow is already half raised, it feels sloppy. The viewer is cheated out of seeing the change in reaction. If The Thing is a camera move that's already moving when you cut to it, it will usually feel jarring.

Let's break this down further with a follow-up to **RULE #13 (Guide the viewer's eye with sequential attention magnets)** as you choose the exact beginning of your shot:

Motion is one of the strongest attention magnets of all. Plus, depending on your previous shot, the viewer's eyes are going to be scanning the frame so their brain can decide where to focus attention. That process takes time, even if only a split second.

If your next shot begins with a fast motion that's already happening

THE SINGLE EDIT

before the viewer's eyes are locked in, they'll miss part of it, the edit will feel incomplete, and the viewer will feel cheated. They may not even be able to verbalize it, but they will absolutely feel that something's not quite right.

The solution: give the viewer enough time for their eyes to stop wandering around the frame.

If you're moving to a shot with fast action already in process, keep the outpoint of outgoing Shot A the same, but add an extra 3 to 6 frames at the beginning of incoming Shot B. That way your viewers' eyes will have that split second to lock in to what you want them to see in Shot B. And that means the edit is much more likely to feel smooth and invisible to the viewer.

Then on the flip side: when ending a shot, make a deliberate choice. Don't just say "I guess we'll end it…. here?"

Bad editor. No cookie for you.

Once The Thing finishes, get out of the shot. If the pacing of the shots around the edit point is relaxed, you can get out slowly. If the surrounding parts are moving quickly, get out of the shot immediately, maybe even cutting off a few last frames of The Thing.

But if the shot is at the end of a scene, other factors can affect the out point. You have to ask yourself, "Does this end point feel right? Does it make sense?"[20]

Whatever you choose for the beginning or end of your shot, make it an active choice. Do it *on purpose*.

---

20   For more on this idea of how and when to adjust the outgoing timing of shots, see **RULE #25** (Think of transitions like you're writing a novel).

EDIT BETTER

RULE #22 | USE PAUSES IN AUDIO OR DIALOGUE TO TRIGGER CUT POINTS.

In general, scripted film or TV projects are less likely to have editing that's driven by voiceover or off-screen dialogue. In the non-scripted world, though, you have many projects whose editorial backbone is voiceover or narration. This could be a reality TV show featuring a main character who narrates the scene, on and off-camera. It could be a news piece with the show's host narrating the package. Most news pieces begin and end with an on-camera reporter doing a standup, then use off-camera voiceover in the middle. Or perhaps you're editing a marketing video that is just black words on a white page, voiceover, and that's it.

Whatever the case, when audio or voiceover drives the content of the piece in question, it's almost always safe to use breaks in the voiceover or audio to trigger visual edit points. Punctuation breaks and pauses in phrasing are easy targets.

Take this voiceover track for example: *Last night in Hollywood, the stars were out in full force for the premiere of this year's most over-publicized blockbuster ever, "Snow White vs. Godzilla 7."*

Talk about a killer franchise. But I digress. Edit points for this amazing narration might go like this:

[3-SECOND FLASHY MONTAGE CUT TO MUSIC] Last night in Hollywood,

[CUT] the stars were out in full force [This line gets 3-4 shots of famous people] for the premiere of this year's

[CUT] most over-publicized

[CUT] blockbuster ever,

INTRODUCTION

[CUT] "Snow White vs. Godzilla 7."

[Show movie poster, then CUT TO famous people on the red carpet talking about how amazing they are in this amazing movie].

If you think this sounds like a lot of cuts for such a small amount of narration, you'd be right. But that's how it's done. If you haven't recently, watch an episode of an entertainment news show and you'll see this is the pace they use. And it's the pace the viewing public has come to expect. Other projects might require a slower pace, but the cut points still fall between narration phrases, punctuations, and sentences.

RULE #23 | BE AWARE OF ON-CAMERA SUBJECTS BLINKING WHEN CUTTING.

Does it seem like I'm talking a lot about people blinking? Maybe so. It's a big deal. Here's more about it.

Editing has many similarities to carrying on a conversation in person. You look at a person when you're talking to them, then at some point you look away to something else. This process of shifting from one point of focus to another shows up visually when people blink. They say something, or shift their vision to another place, then blink. It's even more obvious when they are on camera. People blink before they begin a sentence, after they finish a sentence, or when they switch mentally to a different thought.

Never noticed this? Start looking for it – it happens constantly.

For editing, on-camera blinking becomes important when choosing your cut points. As discussed in **RULE #11 (Read Walter Murch's *In the Blink of an Eye* to understand why editing works at all)**, editing performs the same function as blinking. Viewers understand this, if only subconsciously.

Because of this, it feels odd when an on-camera subject blinks too closely to an edit point. The audience experiences a "double blink" – one visual, and one electronic, and people instinctively know that something's wrong. The blink and its electronic equivalent are a psychologically rooted function of communicating, and when you mess with putting them too close together, it feels weird.

In fact, I'm just gonna say it's flat-out wrong.

Don't do it!!

Just so we're clear, it's perfectly fine to show someone blinking while on camera. It can be an expressive mode of communication and can sometimes be hysterically funny. There can be good reasons to show someone blinking or fluttering their eyes on-camera. Just make sure it doesn't happen too close to the beginning or end of the shot.

RULE #24 | PUT YOUR EDIT POINT EXACTLY ON THE BEAT OF A MUSIC TRACK ONLY IF YOU WANT TO EMPHASIZE THE EDIT ITSELF.

Years ago, I edited a music video with shots of the artists walking down sidewalks and alleys until they ran into each other. The song was a moody, hipsterish track, and I started experimenting with jump cuts of the artists walking on specific beats of the music track. It worked pretty well, and both the director and I were happy.

Unfortunately, for a while after cutting that video, I relied too heavily on this device. What worked well for a hipster music video looked clunky in other contexts. And time after time, amateur and professional editors alike try to "give the piece more energy" and "add some flash" by editing right on the music beats. Sometimes it works, but often it doesn't.

THE SINGLE EDIT

Why? Because **placing edits directly on music hits calls attention to the edit.**

This raises a question that goes far beyond editing to music: Do you want your audience to notice the edit?

Like many of life's questions, this one is hard to answer with a simple "yes" or "no." Most times, I want my editing to be invisible. I don't want anything to distract from the message I want to communicate.

Having said that, there are times when our task is to present something in an engaging, energetic way, but the subject matter is not at all exciting. Like a cornfield. (Having grown up in Iowa, I assure you that cornfields are anything but riveting.) In that case, I might add extra edits to the beats of the music and behold! The Cornfield of AWESOMENESS.

So yes, there are special cases where you want to call attention to your edit. More often than not, though, you will want to keep the edit point off the beat and let the action do the talking.

TRANSITIONS:
Getting from Here to There

Transitions function on two main levels: the big scale and the small scale.

The big scale ties into the structure of your editing. What are the ideas, how do they flow, and how do your transitional devices between ideas move things along?

Then of course we're all familiar with transitions on the small scale going from shot to shot. Fades, dissolves, and all those nutty, flip-flopping, 3D edge wipe digital gimmick thingies. But transitions don't have to be crazy, computer-generated wipes to do their thing. If you get right down to it, we're moving things along from here to there every single time we make a straight cut.

Transitions link ideas together and move them forward, backward, and sideways.

Let's talk about that.

EDIT BETTER

RULE #25 | THINK OF TRANSITIONS LIKE YOU'RE WRITING A NOVEL.

Think of yourself as Ernest Hemingway.[21] Or if you don't like the idea of depression leading to suicide, think of yourself as some other well-known book-writing type.

Consider the structure of a written novel. Novelists know, and editors know, that your project is comprised of big ideas, like chapters. Those chapters are made up paragraphs, paragraphs are made up of sentences, and sentences are strung together with punctuation.[22]

This structure lives in the big scale and the small scale at the very same time. In the big picture, everything begins with a progression of ideas. Writers and video editors alike consider **RULE #6** **(Understand the piece before you begin)** and **RULE #9** **(Find the backbone of your piece and hang everything on it).**

So to further apply Rule #6 within the context of transitions, the effective communicator asks, "Does the overall flow of ideas make sense?" Do the ideas show a natural progression, or do they just kind of sit awkwardly, sort of working but sort of not?

Here's the cool thing: **the communicator who shapes ideas on the big scale actually makes them happen by the effective use of transitions on the small scale.**

The mechanics of moving through a flow of big-picture ideas in a novel happens by the application of sentences, words, and punctuation – periods, semicolons, exclamation points, etc.

---

21   *Follow-up to* **RULE #15** (Seek simplicity by highlighting only what's important): *Ernest Hemingway was famous for his minimalist prose. Stories tell of his making a wager with friends where they bet he couldn't write an entire story in 6 words. His response, scribbled on a napkin: "For sale: baby shoes, never worn."*
22   *Unless you're James Joyce. Or most people on Facebook.*

TRANSITIONS: GETTING FROM HERE TO THERE

The video editor does the exact same thing. The actual nuts and bolts of moving the big picture forward in an edit happens with the punctuation of picture and sound editing – fades, dissolves, cuts, and the occasional flashy digital transition thingy (more on those in a bit).

As a video editor, consider written punctuation as a model for editorial punctuation:

• Do you want to end in a period? End your scene with a brief pause, and a straight cut to whatever comes next.

• Do you want to end with ellipses and have your idea just kind of peter out like this…? Use a medium or long fade or dissolve.

• Do you want to end with an exclamation point? Keep the timing very tight at the end of your shot, and get out with a straight cut, or maybe a flare or flash transition. Even better to include some sort of sound effect with it too.

Of course, we editors have tools at our disposal to communicate transitions of thought that novelists don't.

• Timing: ending a major section or the entire piece often affects the timing of your editorial punctuation – generally speaking, adding more time for the last shot to sit there or disappear from the screen.

• Dissolves are typically – but not always – used to show a passage of time. They can be equally effective in combining ideas simultaneously without reference to time passage.

• Content-based transitions or editorial style choices. More on this in a bit.

So that's the general strategy of transitions – while they certainly are connecting devices between shots, they're also catalysts in the progression of ideas.

RULE #26 | MINIMIZE THE USE OF FANCY DIGITAL TRANSITIONS.

When I was in high school, we didn't have Final Cut or iMovie. Premiere was in its infancy, and Avid cost over $100,000 for one system. The thing I did have access to: a state-funded editing suite in a town an hour away from where I lived in Northwest Iowa. While I mainly edited on the suite's linear VHS cuts-only editing systems, occasionally I got to work with the "high-end" system called the Video Toaster. It didn't run on a Mac or a PC – it ran on a computer platform called the Amiga (which no longer exists).

I was in awe of this system that controlled S-VHS video decks by punching in timecodes on a computer. My supervisor told me that one of the first things people always did when they set up a Video Toaster system was to start playing with all the menus of shot transitions.

Some of the transitions were fairly straightforward – dissolves, wipes, and fades – but some were kinda funky. One of them, for example, was the silhouette of a basketball player. The shadowy figure entered from screen right while dribbling the basketball and threw it straight at the screen. The basketball shadow filled up the screen and dropped down, revealing the next shot. I actually used that one for a video for my high school's basketball team, because in that case it actually made sense.

But some of those transitions made you wonder how on earth could anyone ever use them. There was one where, once you triggered the transition, you heard, "Baaaa! Baaaa!" And then wool-coated cartoon sheep fall from the top of the screen, pile on top of each other, and fly back into the sky to reveal the next shot. All the while going, "Baaaa! Baaaa!"

TRANSITIONS: GETTING FROM HERE TO THERE

As you can tell, it left an impression on me.

It was amazing to think that someone designed such an effect, and even more amazing to think that someone would actually use it. I mean, really? Flying sheep? After that, whenever we had a project where there hadn't been enough planning, we'd say, "Better pull out the flying sheep for this one." It's become verbal shorthand for dressing a piece up by artificial means to hide the fact that there's not enough content. This happens all the time, even at the highest levels in Hollywood.

Overuse of transitions can signal to your audience that you're trying to hide something. They may not be able to verbalize it, but it will feel like eating three bags of cotton candy – you ate a lot but you're not full.

And now, an exception. There is indeed content where flashy digital transitioning literally *is* the content – specifically entertainment news, of which I've cut more than I care to admit.[23] If the whole style of the material is "Show graphic in, swish pan wipe, white flash, 3D cube spin to floating still over fast-motion backplate, star wipe out to a show graphic," then by all means do it.

There are times when your overseers/director/producers will want some flashy stuff, but for the rest of the time most people want things to stay fairly clean. Cuts, fades, etc.

---

23 Entertainment news is an interesting animal. You get into the bay at 7 a.m., start cutting a piece that will only air once, streams live to millions of people later that day… who promptly forget they ever saw it. If you're an adrenaline junkie who's just in it for the deadline-driven madness, it can be quite a rush. But if you're looking to create something that provides lasting value to the world, well… ya may want to consider something other than stories about red carpet.

EDIT BETTER

When digital transitions work best

Digital transition elements are most effective when you're showing a clear change of section or idea. For instance, if you're editing a game show and the host says, "Now, let's learn a little bit more about contestant X." That's the cue for the transition to fly by with a "whoosh!" Then you see a background piece of the gal talking about herself. Once she's finished, "Whoosh!" Use that same transition and sound effect, and you're back to your on-camera host.

Or in the scripted world, sometimes digital swish pans or picture pushes can be used between scenes to clearly tell the audience "hey, we're moving on here."

You wouldn't ever put a 3D spinning wipe between Shot 1 and Shot 2 for no good reason. It would feel out of place. Nine out of ten times, you'll want to use a straight cut. But when you want to specifically point out a change of idea to your audience, transitional devices can work well.

RULE #27 | MAKE SURE THE TRANSITION DOESN'T STEP ON ANYTHING IT SHOULDN'T.

One of the things I see all the time (that I wish I didn't) is a fancy transition without any space between Shot 1 and Shot 2. The editor left the timing between the shots the same as if there was no additional connecting element, but he still just smacked the transition right on top.

Not cool.

You want to make sure there's enough time and space for your transition (and sound effect, if applicable) to live in its own space. It should not visually or sonically step on any endings or beginnings of words people are saying on screen.

TRANSITIONS: GETTING FROM HERE TO THERE

> **RULE #28** | **STRETCH YOUR CREATIVITY TO MAKE IDEAS FLOW WITHOUT VISUAL CRUTCHES.**

There are times when a graphic-driven transition is the best solution for a specific moment in your edit. And it's awfully easy to slap a couple sections of your piece together with a flash or a fancy wipe. But let's face it: only rarely do those transitions require much in the way of true creativity. Why not use the actual elements of your piece to make the ideas move even more naturally without visual gimmicks?

Here are some ideas:

• Content-based transitions. Timelapse footage is a great way to show time passing, be it sun or moon moving across the sky, the hands of a clock spinning wildly, or a daytime city moving into its brightly lit night lighting. You can also show the obvious changing of seasons to indicate passage of time. Even better, you can show one certain place or activity happening in the exact same way with the only difference being spring rain, summer sun, fall colored leaves, winter snow, etc. One quirky movie used this idea in showing a high school track team running around the same track in all the different seasons to show passage of time.[24] The filmmakers did not use a clock wipe to get in and out of those shots. They didn't need to.

• Editorial style. Reality television loves to lock off a little camera with its birds-eye view high above the scene, and set it to rolling for the next 24 hours.[25] That footage can either be sped up and used as standard timelapse footage to show passage of time, or the editor can more directly use a series of jump cuts, often cut to the beat of a music cue, to show unfolding process. Compression

---

24   Juno, *2007*.
25   *Most often used in shows involving building, remodeling, or other obviously visual progression over time. Classic example:* Extreme Makeover: Home Edition *(2003-2012).*

of process can even be represented by three or four half-second shots sequenced together rapid-fire. All of a sudden a character has slammed down a phone, jumped on an airplane and burst into an office in person halfway around the world in literally three seconds of screen time.[26] That extreme kind of abbreviation won't work for every project, but it just might work for yours.

• Sound work. One slick way of moving from one idea to another: when outgoing scene A ends, start fading in some continuous sound other than dialogue from incoming scene B. Fade that in under the outgoing picture of scene A, and you can just cut straight to scene B. The transition has been accomplished by doing an audio dissolve that signals the audience, "Here's the next thing that's coming up."[27]

• Transitions can be accomplished with music too. Music is often a key element of moving from one idea to the next. It can be as simple as editing your music so that it obviously ends as the scene ends. Then when you cut to the next scene, you can start a new music cue at the beginning of the next shot. Or even better, have the music react to an opening line of dialogue in the next scene. More about music in a bit.

---

26   *Used in quickly paced action-driven movies like* Snatch *(2000).*
27   *A regular technique used by Walter Murch in movies like*
The Conversation *(1974).*

TRANSITIONS: GETTING FROM HERE TO THERE

Recap

Say the word "transition" to many editors, and they will instantly think of fancy digital wipe things. But really, the purpose of those fancy shot transitions goes beyond getting from Shot A to Shot B… transitions are about the movement of ideas. And as mentioned above, that can be done in all sorts of ways that may involve nothing more than the content of your project and straight cuts.

MUSIC:
Select, Place, Arrange

Music is a subject near and dear to my heart. For the bulk of my life, I've been known as "Jeff the Piano Guy" because I've played piano since I was four. At one point, I even considered becoming a concert pianist – thankfully I came to my senses and pursued a path where I could actually make a living without spending 10 hours a day locked in a practice room.[28][29] But I kept at it through high school, and by the time my senior recital came around I could play all sorts of heavy classical stuff. I put my hand to composing, arranging, and recording starting in junior high, and studied music composition in college. So music has always been a huge part of my life.

When I came out to Los Angeles to pursue editing, I played less and less piano. People thought I had given up on music, and for a while it felt like I had. But as I moved up from the technical roles of assisting to the creative work of editing, I realized that my

---

28   Hey, what's the difference between a professional musician and a large pizza? The pizza can feed a family of four.
29   Ironically, I now spend 10 hours a day in a small room as an editor. Hmmm.

knowledge of the elements and performance of music were a huge advantage in communicating powerfully with editing.

Countless producers and executives have told me that the best editors they've ever worked with are musicians in one form or another. The thing is, music can be downright mystifying if you don't know how to work with it.

Music editing follows three main phases. This actually applies to editing in general, but specifically to music:

SELECT, PLACE, ARRANGE.

You – assuming it's you and not a music supervisor or composer – first need to decide which pieces of music you want and why, then you place them in your sequence, and in that process of placement, you end up reworking or tweaking the music, picture, or both.

SELECTING MUSIC

> **RULE #29** — TREAT MUSIC AS A CHARACTER EQUAL TO ANYTHING OR ANYONE IN YOUR PIECE.

As you begin the selection of your music, you first need to acknowledge that music is actually important, that it matters. You would not *believe* how many people, including regularly working professional editors don't.

As an assistant editor itching to do more editing, I once asked an editor how to edit music. He said, "Oh, that's easy. You just drop it in."

Uhh… okay. Not helping.

I've since observed that many editors hold to a philosophy – and even if they say otherwise, actions speak louder than words – that music is

MUSIC: SELECT, PLACE, ARRANGE

just a thing that you drop into your timeline, and it just sits there like beige wallpaper blandly adhering to the wall of your kitchen.

STOP IT.

MUSIC IS NOT WALLPAPER, DAMMIT.

If you treat music as just a random thing to slap into your piece, your piece will suck. At the very least, it will fall short of the impact it could have made otherwise. How do I know this? I have built my career in Hollywood fixing the work of other editors who treat music like wallpaper.

When used well, music possesses an entire range of emotions and energies that can take your piece to places it could never otherwise go. Let the music strut, whisper, or shout as it should. Sometimes it mumbles in the background, sometimes it chatters out front, and sometimes it gets in your face and smacks you upside the head.

Now if it's supposed to be in the background, then let it sit there and leave it alone. But if it's supposed to say something, whether subtly or up in your face, let it do it. And when you do, don't put other audio elements like dialogue over it. That would dilute the power of what the music is saying. Unless, of course, that's what you're going for.

RULE #30 | FACTOR IN EXPECTATIONS WHEN SELECTING MUSIC.

So now that you're respecting music as the critical player it is, how do you narrow down the choices of which cue of music to actually use in your piece?

It begins by balancing expectations, taking us back to **RULE #3** (Determine your Market) and **RULE #5** (Determine your Method).

EDIT BETTER

Who is your Market, your Audience for your piece? This may not be as straightforward as it seems. If you're the sole decision-maker on your project, then you need to look downstream and say, "Who will be seeing this, and how will that affect my music choices?"

But if you are answering to a creative partner, director, producer, or client, guess what? THEY are your first audience. Maybe not the ultimate end viewing audience, but nine out of ten times you will have to pick music that makes *them* happy first.

If you're cutting a documentary on Kurt Cobain and your director wants to score the piece exclusively with Beethoven sonatas, then it doesn't matter if your end audience still wears flannel and hates anything that doesn't smell like teen spirit… you'd better start pulling up the classical piano section of your music library.[30]

So once you know who you need to please, ask yourself, "What do they expect?" That will start to shape your music choices.

You can also ask, "What do they *not* expect?" This is a great starting point if you're building comedy. Suppose you have a shot of a little girl walking down the street. People might typically expect happy little girl music. If you take that same shot and put in music that sounds like a showdown at the OK Corral, well, that's not something most people would expect. And when the audience expects one thing but gets another, it often ends up funny. Sometimes really funny.

---

30   This does not mean that you can't question your director's sanity. Directors are not always known to be the most sane people in town. Having said that, remember **RULE #20** (Be willing to experiment) – *seriously, you never know when some seemingly ludicrous idea will create magic.*

MUSIC: SELECT, PLACE, ARRANGE

> **RULE #31** | **WHEN IN DOUBT, CHOOSE MUSIC THAT EXAGGERATES YOUR PIECE'S EXISTING EMOTION.**

There is a very unique feeling of satisfaction when you find the perfect piece of music for a certain moment. It just feels right, and you know it in your gut. At times you may be selecting your music and not know what that "just right" fit is. In those times, here's how to move forward: decide what the piece's existing emotion is, and look for music cues that will make it more extreme. Yes, you're ultimately looking for "just right" – but then I go back to the whole wallpaper thing:

So many people treat their music like wallpaper, and their pieces die horrible, boring deaths as a result.

Listen. People watch TV, movies, and videos for all kinds of reasons. And for every *one* person who watches because they want nothing more than to learn new information, you have *fifty* people who watch because they want to feel something. Acknowledge that emotional need of the audience. Use your music choices to make the emotion more extreme. Don't be satisfied with creepy, ridiculous, or sad; aim for *nail-bitingly* creepy, *absurdly* ridiculous, or *heartstoppingly* sad.

For instance, if you have a scene about a guy that just got dumped by his girlfriend, and the point is to show that he's sad, you can't expect to achieve that by using some bland cue that says, "Aww, I'm kinda bummed."

No.

The music needs to feel as if the guy just witnessed the dog that he's known since childhood die in his arms after being fatally hit by a Mack truck, then he went back to his apartment only to discover that the fridge no longer contains a single bottle of beer, and THEN the guy's girlfriend walked into the room, reached into his rib cage, ripped his heart out, and stomped on it with six-inch stiletto heels.

I'm talking soul-crushing, "point me to the nearest window so I can jump" kind of sadness here.

Now is it possible that scoring your music to emotional extremes will sound overdone? Absolutely. But it's much more likely that it will be just right. Why can I say this? Because after an entire career doing this in Hollywood, I still experience that very phenomenon all the time. Here's why:

If you've ever taken acting classes, or done much auditioning for singing, on-camera, or voiceover roles, you have probably offered a performance or a take that prompts the director to say "Okay, let's bring that one certain thing out more." You do it again, and the director isn't happy. "No, I'm talking much more." And you take the performance to the point where you feel physically uncomfortable, and your brain is telling you "what the heck, this is WAY over the top!" And when you do, the director grins and says, "YES! That's it!" And you realize that you just got coached into a really powerful performance because you had to push things further than you initially wanted to.

Whether in performance or editing, if your choices are playing too strongly, you can always dial them back. Otherwise step out there and take a risk. Because that's when you experience breakthroughs. That's when your performance or your edit goes to places it would never have otherwise gone. And it's because you had the guts to push things to a place that initially felt too extreme… but very often ends up being "just right."

MUSIC: SELECT, PLACE, ARRANGE

PLACING MUSIC

You've made some initial choices for pieces of music to go into your piece. The next question is, where in the timeline does the music go?

RULE #32 | DECIDE WHETHER THE MUSIC IS ACTING OR REACTING.

When in a conversation, we find ourselves in a constant state of shifting between two states: Acting and Reacting. We might walk up to a person and make a statement that begins an exchange. We are Acting by making that opening statement, and the other person Reacts to us with their response.

Music does the exact same thing. It is perfectly comfortable stepping out front at the beginning of the scene and saying "Welcome to the show, everyone. Here's what this scene is about!" It is equally comfortable letting the scene begin, having something happen, then stepping in (or maybe sneaking in) to say, "Here is how you should feel about what just happened."

Depending on the desired effect, music might begin the scene or piece by Acting, and then change energy or sections at different times as a way of Reacting.

Either way, the important thing is that you, the editor, decide what function the music will perform – in effect, a miniature version of **RULE #1** (**Determine your Desired Outcome**) specifically for the music cue in question. This will not only help you select the right music to begin with, but it will further inform your decision of exactly when to start, stop, or change the music. The next rule takes that idea even further.

EDIT BETTER

RULE #33 | USE MUSIC TO BEGIN, END, OR CHANGE IDEAS.

I didn't know it at the time, but the young assistant editor version of myself who asked "How do you actually edit music," was actually asking "How do you know when to stop or start the music?"

Aha! Out of the 87,000 editing-related questions whose answers all end up being "it depends," this question actually has a pretty straightforward answer:

Music begins, ends, or changes in conjunction with a shift in ideas.

Unfortunately, the best way to really clarify and cement this idea in your head is to hear it in an edited sequence, not read words in a book. When you hear a well-crafted shift in music in conjunction with good editing, you get it, it just makes sense. Given the limitations of this book, let's explain further.

Consider the workings of your car. Whether automatically or at your direction, your car's transmission is constantly shifting gears up and down depending on the speed of your engine and the speed your car is traveling. Sometimes you're in neutral, and the engine is barely running at all. Other times if you live in Los Angeles (or other city with heavily congested traffic), you're on the freeway literally creeping forward at seven miles per hour in first gear for half a mile. And other times you're flying along, upshifting and downshifting as you skid around hairpin curves on a closed racetrack.[31]

---

31 *I recently had the opportunity to drive a Lamborghini on a closed course under the direction of a professional racing instructor. If you have never experienced being pinned back in your seat as you floor the accelerator of a $200,000 Italian supercar – that YOU'RE driving – I cannot recommend it highly enough. I've done rollercoasters and skydiving... and they're just not the same thing. Very few things compare to that jolt of adrenaline. It's absolutely insane.*

MUSIC: SELECT, PLACE, ARRANGE

Editing is the same way. Your piece is constantly shifting conceptual gears up and down through beginnings, endings, and shifts of emotion, thought, or sections. Any number of those points of change can be good triggers for a corresponding beginning, internal change, or end of your music.

ARRANGING MUSIC

In my junior high school years, I started fiddling with electronic keyboards, MIDI sequencers, and tape recorders, learning how different instruments interact with others. I remember preferring to put my own spin on an existing song (arranging) instead of writing a brand new one (composing). Years later, I found myself thinking the same thing as I realized how much I enjoy shaping elements someone else had shot (editing) instead of creating my own piece from scratch (writing or directing).[32]

In music terminology, editing is much more like arranging than composing. Editors take existing elements and shape them into a collective whole, just as music arrangers put their own twist on existing melodies and chord progressions.

And guess what? The role of the video editor constantly involves actual arranging of music too.

---

32   This is an important distinction if you're looking to make a career in the music or entertainment industries. The bulk of the money and fame go to content creators. How many music arrangers can you name off the top of your head compared to music composers or songwriters? How many famous video or film editors can you list compared to TV or film directors? Those who edit and arrange perform a valuable service and can often be well compensated for it. But the potential for fame and the really big money is much more heavily weighted towards those who create the script or the song in the first place.

RULE #34 | FIT THE MUSIC TO THE PIECE, NOT THE PIECE TO THE MUSIC.

Let's be clear about something:

As editor, the music exists to be in service to **you**. It can offer you suggestions about what might work here or there, but ultimately you are the one shaping it, not vice versa.

Why do I say this? Because of all the times I hear people say, "Well, the song is five minutes long, so I have to make this section of the piece to fit the music."

No. You don't.

Especially not if the content matter you're cutting will only hold the audience's attention for two minutes. Anything after that, you're in the process of alienating your audience, even if they're too polite to say so.

Now even though the music is your slave, this is not to say that you can't shift parts of your piece to better fit with the music – you definitely should. And this took me a while to figure out.

At one point a number of years ago I was sitting in a room on the backlot of Universal Studios learning about the skills of the film assistant editor. It wasn't yet obvious that physical film was dead, and I figured it could be worthwhile to learn more about the process of working with physical film.

Film post-production is a much more complex, multi-role process than most television or video post. My only point of reference at the time was watching the TV editors who were responsible for editing all picture, all sound, and all the music. I knew that they regularly tweaked picture elements to fit more closely to the music, and it sounded really difficult for that to happen with the film editorial process that was being described.

MUSIC: SELECT, PLACE, ARRANGE

I raised my hand and asked the teacher, a retirement-aged man who'd been splicing and dicing film workprint for 40 years, "Do music supervisors or composers ever ask you to change picture elements to fit the music better?"

"No," he growled, "I tell them, 'Change one frame and I'll kill you.'"

Well then. Very different world here.

To rephrase what I believe he meant, and what I've since learned: editing process that involves multiple editors working on multiple areas of the piece (picture, dialogue, sound effects, music) requires a very specific workflow. Changes can be made, but you have to follow a set process to do that.

In the TV and video world, things are much easier because usually there's only one editor – you – doing everything. If you lay in a piece of music with a specifically chosen beginning point, and there's a great turn in the music within a second of a place where an editorial shift of thought should happen, then by all means consider shifting picture elements to more accurately synchronize with the music shift.

Mix and match picture, sound, and music elements to fit together the best way possible. Your piece will be all the better for it.

RULE #35 | ALTER THE MUSIC MOST EFFECTIVELY BY PRESERVING ESTABLISHED PATTERNS.

So at this point you've chosen your music cue, you've considered how it will function in your sequence, and where you might want it to start, stop, or change. You may now be thinking, "I have the perfect piece of music, but I think it needs to be shortened or chopped up in different parts – how do I do that?"

That is a whole set of skills in and of itself. And a book falls woefully short explaining in words what takes place conceptually via the altering of sound.

Here's the beginning of an explanation here:

As stated earlier in **RULE #12** **(Actively direct the viewer's attention)**: Your brain is a giant sorting machine with the one goal of making sense of the world and all the inputs the world throws at it. It wants to put everything into categories and boxes and compare what it gets with what it expects.

Music is chock full of patterns, and our brains LOOOVE that.[33]

Thing is, the types of sonic patterns that music offers to the world are just as varied as music itself is. Those patterns operate on the big scale of recurring themes, verses, or choruses, and also on the recurring elements of musical measures, single musical beats, or individual notes themselves.[34]

As our brains constantly search for musical patterns in edited pieces, they feel all warm and fuzzy when the music sets up offers of patterns and sticks to them in a way that makes sense and supports the communication of the edited piece. But sometimes those patterns get broken up and our brains say "Hey! HEYY!! I was feeling all comfortable with that pattern, but it just got interrupted!!"

---

33   Irony: as I'm typing this, I'm sitting on a train in downtown Los Angeles on my way to do some editing. A guy just walked on the otherwise quiet train and started blasting rap music out of his phone. The in-your-face rhythmic patterns of the drumbeats were an instant attention magnet to my highly music conscious brain. And when my brain is focusing on that, I find it almost impossible to think about writing. I moved to another train car. Ahh, much better. Wait. Someone else is blasting music through their earbuds. Sigh.
34   For those familiar with different kinds of world music, my comments will apply primarily to Western-based music. Eastern music in its non-Western-tainted form uses a whole different set of ground rules.

MUSIC: SELECT, PLACE, ARRANGE

Behold, a bad music edit.

A bad/rough/sloppy music edit is a violation of a previously established musical pattern.

So as you're going through the music arranging process, you will want to make "good music edits" by maintaining whatever established patterns the music has laid out.

But how does that actually work? It works by knowing the elements of music, just like you know the elements of whatever language you happen to speak – and let's be clear, music IS its own complete language.

You generally wouldn't edit a piece of dialogue to begin with half of the first word missing. But it happens all the time with music – half a beat or a weird fraction of a measure of the song gets lopped off early or hangs too late before the edit point arrives.

And now… a description of ONE way to make an exact music edit.

Just like our discussion of visual transitions (see **RULE #25**, **Think of transitions like you're writing a novel**), musical transitions work on the big scale and the small scale. But even if you're talking going from Big Music Section A to Big Music Section B, you still have to choose an *exact* edit point on the small scale to make that big shift happen. Generally speaking, music is much less forgiving than picture when it comes to making choices for your edit points.

And to many, the process of making a perfect music edit is downright maddening, mystifying, or both. (Or they're blissfully unaware of the need to make good music edits, which means they probably treat music like wallpaper. BAD!!! BAD!!!)

But remember, you already know the big secret of music editing:

Make "good music edits" by maintaining whatever established patterns the music has already laid out.

Time to break it down. Think of it like this: you're at a dance club, and the music is thumping. Literally thumping.

Thump, thump, thump, thump, thump. That low-frequency thump thing present in virtually all dance music is the bass drum. It's the foundation of all the rhythmic patterns the dance music offers up to the brains of anyone within earshot. Sometimes the bass drum is all by itself.

In that case, you can put a musical edit point anywhere you want, as long as the same amount of time between each "thump, thump, thump" is maintained. That's the pattern that our brain expects to continue.

Usually there's lots of stuff layered on top of that bass drum though – let's add in just one more drum element. Whenever you hear someone going "oom-tsss-oom-tsss-oom-tsss-oom-tsss," they're imitating the classic rhythmic pattern of club music that's found in the interplay between the bass drum and cymbals, usually a funky two-pieced cymbal stacked on top of itself called a highhat. The rhythm tracks offer up that pattern that our brains eat up like a kindergartener gobbling up candy bars on Halloween:

Oom-tsss-oom-tsss-oom-tsss-oom-tsss.

Over and over and over.

Now say you want to edit Section B of this dance track to the end of Section A. Section B continues with a slightly different bass drum sound that goes with a "DOM-tsss-DOM-tsss-DOM-tsss" pattern.

You could drop in that incoming section of "DOM-tsss" anywhere you'd come to an "oom" in the outgoing Section A. Because the two

MUSIC: SELECT, PLACE, ARRANGE

sections have the same sort of timing, you just need to match them up with each other:

Oom-tsss-oom-tsss//DOM-tsss-DOM-tsss…

The thing that you must absolutely NOT do is to start the "DOM" section where a "tsss" would normally happen.

Oom-tsss-oom-tsss-oom//DOM-tsss-DOM-tsss…

That would interrupt the bass drum and highhat pattern that your brain has been told to expect. Hence, that interruption would create… a bad music edit.

The above examples use just ONE teensy-tiny strategy for editing ONE kind of music. To say that this only scratches the surface of how to make exact music edits is a monumental understatement.

But honestly, this rule will literally guide you in any music edit you make, anytime, anywhere:

Make "good music edits" by maintaining whatever established patterns the music has already laid out.

And also, another good way to test a music edit: does it sound right to you? Rely on that pattern-loving brain of yours, because it's really good at detecting bumps in the sonic road. There are a gazillion explanations for why a music edit may or may not work in any given scenario, but ultimately it comes down to… does it sound right?

An additional thought: there are times when you will make a music edit that will not be smooth at all, but if it happens underneath another sound element that completely covers it up – say, a transitional whoosh or an explosion – then the music edit may not really matter much. Sometimes the quickest way to make a tricky music edit work is to just plain cover it up under other sound.

RULE #36 | LEAVE MARKERS ON MUSIC CHANGES, HITS, OR ENERGY SHIFTS.

This is a technique that has served me well for years. On any given music cue, there will be certain points where the music stops, starts, or changes. It may be a shift in energy, or a specific musical flourish that you can use to drive your picture edit.

When you come across those, use your editing software to leave a marker (or a locator, or whatever your software uses) on the exact frame of the musical shift. Later on, when you want to use that clip, you can load it back up in your source window and jump to the exact points in the music that you highlighted.

This is especially handy if you use certain tracks regularly, or if you use them during an initial cut, need to replace them, but you know they can be used in the future. Once you become familiar with those tracks and their highlighted moments, you can jump right to the exact frames that you've highlighted and cut the appropriate sections into your edit. It's a powerful thing, and I highly recommend it.

Not exhaustive. Sigh.

I could talk about music and music editing for the rest of this book. But that's not practical, and this book is not meant to be exhaustive on anything.

Backing up to the big picture though: treat music as an integral element of communication. Take special care as you select it, place it, and arrange it. Know how it works, respect it, and use every bit of care in its application as you would in selecting the best performance of an actor who was paid twenty million dollars just to step in front of the camera.

The impact of your editing will improve dramatically when you do.

DIALOGUE

Editing dialogue is an art in and of itself. Those men and women who focus exclusively on dialogue editorial typically do so on feature films or well-budgeted scripted TV dramas. Dialogue editors are specialists who can tweak a dialogue edit down to the sub-frame, and they spend years honing their craft.

In light of **RULE #9** **(Find the backbone of your piece and hang everything on it)**: most of the time, the dialogue in your piece will be the backbone of your project. As such, once you've decided what pieces of dialogue you'd like, you'll almost always want to keep it as clean as humanly possible. Here's how.

EDIT BETTER

RULE #37 | MIX YOUR DIALOGUE TO A CONSISTENT LEVEL.

This isn't to say that you need to do a full-blown audio mix pass before the piece is edited, but I do recommend that you get the dialogue levels dialed in before you start setting any other mix levels. Assuming that the dialogue is indeed the backbone of your piece, all other sound will be mixed in relation to it.

Pick a level on your audio meters for the average dialogue level to hit.[35] It can go above or below occasionally, but in general you should keep it consistent. Always make sure you look at the meters on your editing software because our ears are subjective. Your soundtracks will sound different to you depending on how loud the playback level is in the room, or how much background noise is in the area. So while you absolutely should trust your ears, trust your meters more.

RULE #38 | GET RID OF UNNECESSARY DIALOGUE ELEMENTS AND PAUSES. JUST BECAUSE IT'S THERE DOESN'T MEAN IT SHOULD STAY THERE.

Do everything possible to remove buzzes, clicks and other background noise from the dialogue. If your on-camera subject has an annoying habit of clicking her tongue after she ends a sentence, it's usually a good idea to take that out.

And if the person speaking on camera takes an uncomfortable number of pauses… *get rid of them*. Pull them up and cover the resulting jump cuts with other picture. That might sound like a no-brainer, but there are times when I've taken over sequences edited by fellow pros and they left pauses – lots of them – for no good reason whatsoever. And those pauses were *killing* the pace of the piece.

Exception: sometimes there's a good reason for a pause. If someone

---

35 *For most projects, a good average mixing level for dialogue is -14db digital, occasionally peaking to -12 or -10.*

is talking about how his dad died an untimely death, and he starts to get emotional just sitting there not talking, he's saying something with his emotion. And frankly, those looks, wiping his eyes, and pauses are often much more powerful than any words he may actually say. Leave that kind of stuff in.

The stuff you want to take out is stuff that doesn't help you – verbal tics, space fillers, the "um, ah, you know" stuff. Normally, if a guy is stuttering over his words, you take it out. But sometimes a little stutter or stumble might fit with the way the person actually speaks, so it can enhance the reality of how they sound. Also, it can call attention away from the fact that you just made an audio edit.

Pauses can also affect what an audience thinks about a person. If you want them to think the person is intelligent and well spoken, that will drive how you clean up their dialogue. If you want the audience to think the person on-screen is more on the inarticulate side, leave in more of the "ums" and "ahs."

Does that last idea seem a little sketchy, maybe outright manipulative? Keep reading, it gets better.

> **RULE #39** — EXERCISE YOUR AUTHORITY TO CHANGE AND ALTER WORDS. JUST BECAUSE THEY'RE THERE DOESN'T MEAN THEY SHOULD STAY AS THEY ARE.

While this rule might sound slightly devious, the fact is that we as editors are constantly called upon to alter, reorder, and sometimes outright change what people say.

This book is not a place to discuss the ethics of what we should or should not change. I will propose this, though: the act of changing someone's words is much less important than the reason for changing them, and how the altered words are then used.

Use your power for good, Grasshopper, not for evil.

Having said that, it's surprising how many regularly working professionals are unaware of the possibilities for easily altering portions of dialogue. Feel free to eliminate consonants and force contractions in order to make things work. Put the edit point right in the middle of the word if necessary – yes, it's okay to do that if it ends up sounding good. Many times I've been in an edit session where the producer says, "That part of the phrase doesn't work!" And I say, "Just cut off that part of the word and it'll be fine." The idea of taking out words or reordering words or adding consonants or vowels seldom crosses people's minds, but it works.[36]

Bring on the sleaze

Suppose someone on a reality show says, "I never wanted that," but the producer decides they should say the opposite. Well, it's fairly easy to change it to, "I want that." All you have to do is remove the word "never" and the "-ed" from "wanted." Then "I never wanted that," becomes "I want that." A lot can be done by eliminating words or consonants.

Another example: You're interviewing Jane, the principal of a school, and she says, "Sally is my best friend out of all the teachers here." For whatever reason, you'd rather have her say, "Sally is my best teacher here." So you remove, "friend out of all the," and lop off the "s" at the end of "teachers." Make the audio edit a couple frames earlier, and then tack on the last word.

Before: Sally is my best friend out of all the teachers here.
After: Sally is my best// teacher// here.

---

36   If this sounds like a no-brainer to you, very cool. I assure you, it's not self-evident to everyone.

DIALOGUE

Depending on how distinctly each word is pronounced, you could potentially get really fancy and say:

Sally is// the// best// teacher// here.

Now forget fancy, let's go full-on sleazy Reality TV producer on this puppy. Later on in the interview, Principal Jane says, "The school board doesn't seem to appreciate the gravity of the situation." And even later, when asked about the cramped parking lot that she's been working to obtain licenses from the city to expand: "Over 400 of our students have their own cars, and only 100 of them can park on the school lot. It's just not right."

Your network executives decide that instead of Jane and Sally being friends, they should hate each other's guts. Jane's sentence therefore becomes, as a stitched-together Frankenbite:[37]

Before: Sally is my best friend out of all the teachers here.
Before: The school board doesn't seem to appreciate the gravity of the situation.
Before: ...only 100 of them can park on the school lot. It's just not right.

After: Sally// doesn't seem to appreciate// the teachers here.// It's just not right.

Feeling slimy and cheap? Maybe, maybe not. No matter how you

---

37   *Ah, the time-honored tradition of Frankenbiting. If you're not familiar with the word, it's a combination of "soundbite" and "Frankenstein," the novel written in 1818 by Mary Shelley about a mad scientist who stitched together a monster from pieces of various human corpses. A description that some would consider accurate when applied to Reality TV in general. What can I say, I've cut a fair bit of it myself. But even on the really bad shows the production companies' checks have always cleared. Yes, as much as I love great storytelling, sometimes you just end up taking editing gigs because they come along with paychecks.*

happen to feel about it, Frankenbites like these can be heard on television somewhere literally every hour of every day.

And the thing is: when done well, they sound absolutely real. It's no wonder people who appear on TV shows are blown away by how the show puts words in their mouths that they "never said." Well… technically yes, you did. And you signed a whole stack of contracts and legalese saying that they were allowed to do that to you, whether you realized it or not.

But all that is beside the point: as editors, we will be more effective and more highly valued when we exercise our skills to splice, dice, and flip-flop words to clarify, alter, or completely reverse their intended meanings. For better or for worse.

Less sleazy, just slightly tweaked

Another dialogue technique is to use alternate audio under the picture. Suppose a director says, "I love the way the actor looked on take one, but I can't stand the way he sounds." So you pull the audio from take two and put it under the picture from take one. And then you have a perfect take. Potentially.

This is mostly for scripted projects, because it's rare to have multiple takes of the same thing when there is no script. But even on a non-scripted show, if you don't like the way someone says something, see if they say the same word another time. Then you can grab it from there and punch it in. It's amazing how often that can fix an obnoxious delivery.

Now while we're talking about the words people say, whether in talking head soundbites or in-scene, we also need to be aware of how people communicate ideas on screen without saying any words at all.

DIALOGUE

Specifically on non-scripted material, it's tempting for us as editors to say, "They've come to the end of their phrase, therefore I'll put the outpoint after the end of what they say." But they might add something after speaking. If they smack their leg at the end of a strong thought, show it. If they say something ironic and then raise their eyebrow, show it. Let them show personality visually, especially if they laugh or cry. That speaks strongly to what their thoughts are. Let them show their emotion instead of just telling it.

Rule #40 | BEWARE OF BREATHING.

Obviously, people on camera have to breathe in order to talk. It's often tempting to say, "Breaths are not talking. Therefore, I don't have to worry about them."

But when you take your project into an audio mix, or even just play back your sequence at high volume, everything in your audio tracks is magnified... including the breaths. If you get to that point, and you have made a straight cut in your audio where someone starts taking a breath, you will hear it. People will notice, even if they can't quite put their finger on what they're noticing... and that's bad, given that with all the things you want your audience to pay attention to, non-lifelike breaths will likely never be one of them.

So listen for the breathing. When you place your edit points, if your on-camera subject breathes at the end of a phrase, keep that, but then pick up shot two after they have taken their breath. Start in immediately on the dialogue. Otherwise, you'll hear a double breath. If needed, adjust the picture point backwards to make it work both visually and sonically.

Reality check: if you have lots of sound or music layered under your dialogue, chances are nobody will hear little details of an on-screen character's breathing. Just know that the more sonically exposed the dialogue is, the more attention needs to be paid to it.

Speaking of extra layers of sound…

RULE #41 | SMOOTH OUT DIALOGUE BY ADDING CONTINUOUS SOUND.

We usually strive to keep our dialogue as clean as humanly possible, and most times that involves getting rid of unnecessary sounds. Here's the thing though – what we're actually looking to achieve is sound that is both clean *and* lifelike.

Take a moment to stop for 10 seconds or so and listen intently to where you are right now. I'll wait here.

And we're back. Guaranteed you just heard elements of continuous sound. As I write this, sitting at the kitchen island in my house, it's actually relatively quiet. But still there is continuous sound all around me – birds chirping outside the kitchen window. A clock on the wall quietly ticking. And the slightest hum from the tiny fan pulling cool air through the insides of my laptop. And then there are the non-continuous sounds of cars passing by. My wife turns a page in her book and takes a sip of tea. The dog lets out a sigh of boredom.

Here's an idea that some might find counterintuitive: often a section of dialogue can be made to sound more smooth and lifelike by filling the holes and/or adding more layers of continuous sound to it. Because that's what we're used to hearing in real life.

Patching the holes

Specifically, when you remove sections of audio from dialogue that have obvious background noise in them, you leave a sonic hole that's just begging to be filled. How do you fill it? With sound from that environment... where nobody is talking. It's commonly called "room tone." Let's talk about room tone for a second. Common practice in production is to record 30 seconds of room tone at the end of a scene or interview. You wanna know how many times I've used that specifically recorded room tone in my career?

Exactly zero. Never. Here's why:

Sonic environments are constantly changing. Mic positions change. People on camera move around, changing how the sound of their voices bounce back and forth. So by the time a scene or interview is done shooting, the sound at the end will almost *never* sound like the sound in the middle or the beginning. Plus, you may never even find out that they shot room tone until long after you've finished cutting the piece.

So what you will most likely end up doing is hunting for sections of silence near or around the place in the source material which has been partially cut into your sequence. By patching that section of silence into your cut, you are creating your own room tone. Now for sure, that's easier said than done at times. Sometimes there just isn't any decent chunk of spare space. At times, I literally cobble together multiple half-second chunks of audio to create continuous room tone.

Beyond room tone

To reiterate something I said earlier: when it comes to editing dialogue and sound in general, we're actually looking to achieve sound that is both clean *and* appropriately lifelike.

The gold standard by which most dialogue is measured is the dialogue from feature films and scripted TV. The world can literally be coming to an end all around the characters, but incredibly we can

GRAPHICS AND TITLES

This is not a chapter on graphic design, motion design, or typography. While it does touch on some of that, the following ideas focus more on how those subjects all fit into the bigger picture of editing.

Here we go.

RULE #42 — WHATEVER YOU DO, USE ANY FONT OTHER THAN THE DEFAULT FONT.

You may very well be sabotaging your work and not even know it. Whenever you create a new text page or title in your editing software, you are given an option for which font you want to use – Final Cut Pro uses Lucida Grande, and Avid uses Geneva, for a couple examples. If you don't make any changes, your title will be generated using that default font.

You do NOT want that. That is BAD. Here's why.

These default fonts are so insufferably bland and without character that they can literally be used for anything, which is why they were set as default in the first place. Do you *really* want to present your work with elements that are indistinguishable from everything else like it? If so, skip to the next rule. If not, keep reading.

Default fonts aren't just boring. Displaying a title that uses the default font setting practically shouts unspoken messages to anyone who sees it. Either "this person doesn't care enough about details to purposely choose anything other than the default"… or "this person doesn't *know how* to use anything other than the default"…

… both of which are BAD.

Not long ago, some friends of mine produced a beautiful, engagingly shot short film with professional actors, crew, and gear. The filmmakers put together an action-packed trailer that set the scene, built to a crescendo… and… faded up plain, white, unevenly spaced titles in Lucida Grande.

I physically cringed when I saw it. Because literally by virtue of their font choice, my friends had lumped themselves together with

GRAPHICS AND TITLES

every clueless amateur who knows so little about the editing software, *they don't even know how to change the freaking font.*

Sadly, this happens on the big scale too. Some time ago my wife and I were watching a $200 million dollar Hollywood movie that was everything you'd expect for that production budget. Big action scenes, big-name stars, exotic locations. No expense was spared on any detail. Except one glaring one. At one point the film was featuring a beautiful aerial shot flying across a huge city. The filmmakers faded up the name of the city in a title in the lower corner… and it was the most bland, boring, non-choice of a font possible.

I mean, this thing was glaringly, astoundingly plain, dropped right into the middle of a Hollywood blockbuster that otherwise dripped detail and intent with every frame.

Turns out I wasn't the only person who noticed this. An amateur font designer tweeted the film director saying, "Hey, next time you direct a huge Hollywood movie, let me know and I'll provide you with a font that doesn't suck." The director actually replied, saying "If you ever direct a huge Hollywood movie, chances are font choices won't be the most pressing issue on your mind. I chose the first font that I didn't hate."

Now I'm not here to second-guess this director – he's well established and highly respected. Yet the fact remains: an off-the-cuff decision of the first font option that he "didn't hate" remains one of the primary things I actually remember about the movie. Even more than the plot.

"Hey now, relax," you might say. "I happen to like the look of Lucida Grande in my titles."

Yeah, that doesn't matter. Even if you for some weird reason do like Lucida Grande, choosing it instantly puts you in the same category

EDIT BETTER

with people who either don't care or don't know how to change the font to anything else.

Which, actually, is the solution, the golden rule for all titles and graphics for all people in all places for all time:

Whatever you do, use any font other than the default font. Literally *any* other font.[38]

Make your editorial choices on purpose.

> **RULE #43** | **A GRAPHIC OR TITLE IS A VISUAL EVENT AND SHOULD BE TREATED AS SUCH.**

I've often seen professional editors spend all their time thinking about where to place the picture and music edits, but shoot themselves in the editorial foot with the entrances and exits of graphics. They pay great attention to the direction of the audience's eye with pictures, but forget that titles affect the direction of the audiences' eye as well.

"Eh, we'll just put the title… HERE," says an editor. Or worse, a well-meaning assistant editor who doesn't realize the power he wields.

Titles and graphics are not just "slap 'em in" extras. They are Things in and of themselves.

Revisiting **RULE #13** (**Guide the viewer's eye with sequential attention magnets**) – bear in mind that graphics and titles are seriously strong attention magnets, usually because of the words they contain. If you've cut your picture such that your desired focal point is in the upper right section of your screen, and the title

---

38   Except of course for Comic Sans, which should be removed from the face of the earth completely.

GRAPHICS AND TITLES

enters in the lower left section of your screen, your brain will have to rescan and evaluate everything again, possibly feeling a little stuck as to where the most important place is in the screen.

To prevent that, make sure you consider how and when the graphics or titles enter and exit in context with everything else.

RULE #44 | DO NOT FADE A TITLE OUT AT THE END OF A VISUAL CUT.

I often see a title finish a fade out at the exact same time the shot changes. It might seem like a tidy, logical thing to do.

IT'S A TRAP! Don't do it!!

Fading out a title at the same time the shot changes is a virtually guaranteed rough (i.e. bad) edit. Why? Back to **RULE #13 (Guide the viewer's eye with sequential attention magnets)**.

The viewer's brain is confronted with two visual events happening almost at the same time, which means it has to rescan and reevaluate what's important. That takes time, albeit nanoseconds, that distracts from a constant flow of properly sequenced attention magnets.

The smoother way is to have your title or your graphic fade up at the same time as the beginning of the shot. Then, after the audience is done reading it, they will look back up to whatever's happening in the picture. Then the title can fade out. Let it fade before you make another visual cut.

If the initial shot isn't long enough to let that happen, have the title go on halfway into the second or third picture change, then fade out at least half a second before the next cut.

Or you can just have your title fade or reveal on, stay full until the desired edit point, and cut out with the picture cut.

EDIT BETTER

RULE #45 | KEEP SUBTITLES CLEAN AND PRECISE.

Throughout my career, I have not found any consensus about what constitutes universally accepted subtitles. And so I've adopted some specifications that most producers tend to like:

Helvetica, bold (or at least not the skinny version), 28 or 30 points, white fill, 1 point black border with 2 point black shadow, text centered, with the lower edge of the text barely resting on the lower graphic-safe boundary on the bottom of the screen.

Occasionally some shows want something a little edgier than the above specs, but I've used them on almost every show I've ever worked on that uses subtitles.

The care and feeding of subtitles

Overarching idea with the application of subtitles: they, like all other title cards, are visual events. They're already dragging the viewer's eye to the bottom (usually) of the screen to do their thing, so do everything in your power to keep unnecessary visual events to a minimum.

Generally, subtitles should cut on and cut off, no fades needed. Sometimes you might dissolve up or dissolve down, but that's on rare occasions, like when the person is speaking in a slow, thoughtful manner, or if that's the overall style of the editorial treatment. In general though, subtitles should not be fancy. Their point is to cleanly communicate the words being spoken, not call attention to themselves.

For clearest communication, start the subtitle at exactly the same time as the spoken audio, then do whatever possible to end it exactly when the audio ends.

GRAPHICS AND TITLES

If you switch to the next shot right before the on-camera subject finishes her last word, do not extend that subtitle just a handful of frames into the next shot. A subtitle bleeding over into the next shot and disappearing a split second later creates an unnecessary visual event. In that case, either extend the subtitle longer into the next shot or take the subtitle out with the picture change and keep things visually clean.

If the speaker has a pause in their dialogue, don't take down the subtitle unless the pause is significant. For short pauses, just extend the first subtitle until the speaker starts again, and then switch to the next subtitle.

As a general rule, limit subtitles to two lines of text. That way you minimize the amount of work the audience has to do to drag their eyes down the screen.

When deciding how much text will go on each line, split the lines such that one is shorter than the other. If you happen to have three lines of text, make sure the lines are distinctly different lengths from each other. This way the viewer's eye can more easily distinguish between the lines instead of wondering – albeit for a split second – which line starts and ends with which words.

> **RULE #46** | **IF THERE'S A TITLE ON SCREEN, VIEWERS WILL NOT HEAR WHAT'S BEING SAID.**

Our brain puts more weight on what we see than what we hear. So if an image requires extra brain power to comprehend – like a title card – the brain will pay less attention to what is being said, i.e. dialogue or voiceover. I learned this on the first TV show I ever edited, and the lesson applies more than ever today.

Blind Date was a reality dating show that put strangers together on a blind date and followed them around with a camera crew. But the video footage was only half of the show. After the date was shot, the show's writers dreamed up all sorts of captions and cartoon animations to add to the edited segments.

One of the primary devices of the show was the thought bubble, an animated cartoon that would appear on screen containing words that were presumably the thoughts of on-screen characters. Another device was the character-driven lower third title, where a cartoon character popped up with two or three lines of text along the bottom of the screen as commentary from the character.

Example: An especially clueless guy decides to noisily pass gas in the taxicab on the way home. His date is horrified. Lower third pops up: "Dr. Date Says: There's nothing smoother than letting one rip."

Yep, that was the level of humor for a lot of those dates.

The thing we came to realize was that any time those lower thirds or thought bubble titles were on screen, it really didn't matter what the people on the date were saying, or even if they were talking at all. The viewers were too involved in reading the commentary, deciding whether it was funny or not (far from guaranteed), and either laughing or rolling their eyes before turning their attention back to the scene.

During any given dinner scene, the guy might say something. We'd cut to a single shot of the girl listening and taking a drink of wine. Up pops a thought bubble containing whatever thoughts the writers had written. Meanwhile in the scene, the guy continued to talk. We would literally play down the scene for producers and editors who hadn't seen the piece yet and ask them what the guy in the scene said during the time the gal's thought bubble was up. *Nobody could ever remember.*

GRAPHICS AND TITLES

The application? Back to **RULE #43** **(A graphic or title is a visual event and should be treated as such)**, and **RULE #12** **(Actively direct the viewer's attention)**. Our brains lean much more heavily on what is seen than on what is heard. If you have important things that you want your viewer to clearly hear, make sure nothing visual is competing for the viewer's attention.

AUDIO MIXING

Audio mixing is its own art form whose practitioners work for years and years to achieve mastery. And let's just be frank, mixing can be intimidating. Sound mix sessions usually take place on large, ridiculously complicated-looking consoles, and audio engineers speak their own native tongue of odd acoustic phenomena, alien software plug-ins, and random bands that you usually have to enjoy wearing black fingernail polish to ever have heard of them.

I'm the first person to say that if you want your mix to sound really good, you should hire a professional. That's not always an option though. Often when we TV/video editors are expected to be jacks of all the trades, taking a piece to mix isn't in the schedule, budget, or both. So we gotta have half a clue of what we're doing.

And even if you are going to send your piece to be mixed, you still gotta have a mix that works during the editing process (the more solid your temp mix, the better off you'll be selling your editorial ideas).

If you're looking for nuanced details of surround mixing and the secret sauce for mastering in the latest weird formats, you'll need to look elsewhere than this book. Otherwise, here are some ways to get your mix into shape.

RULE #47 | CONSIDER YOUR MIX THROUGH THE PROVERBIAL TELESCOPE.

Where do you start with an audio mix? Would you believe, it's not by setting any levels on anything? Just like viewing our edits through the proverbial telescope, we need to do the same thing with our mix.

Back to a variation on **RULE #1** (**Determine your Desired Outcome**). What do you want as your sonic end result? The answer to this will probably be one of two things:

A final mix, or a temporary mix that does what it needs to until the final mix.

The final mix

Will the sequence that you're editing end up as the final mix for the piece? This happens a lot. You might be putting together a simple little piece to throw out there on YouTube. Or, you might be working on a news or studio-based show where the overall timing doesn't allow for a separate mix, so whatever the offline editor cuts is what goes to air.

If your edit is on behalf of a TV show that puts your mix directly on air, you will usually be told what the general expectations are for mix levels. And the audio engineers on the show will have their gear set to keep audio levels strictly in check.

Otherwise if your edit will represent the final mix, then you need to consider where the final piece is going.

AUDIO MIXING

If it's going somewhere out on the Intarwebs where it needs to stand out, the overall mix needs to be LOUD. As in, as loud as possible without creating distortion – average mix levels up as far as -4 or -2db digital. Find the loudest moment in your piece, and figure out how loud you want it to sit on your audio meters. Mix everything in comparison to that.

If the piece is going somewhere else that doesn't have to be as ridiculously loud, choose your average mix level and stick with that. Most non-film/broadcast video mixes will be fine with average mix levels between -14 to -8db digital. This is a big, sloppy Rule of Thumb. Your piece's requirements may vary.

And if your mix is the final version: **pay attention to details**. Your ears are the ones that have the biggest impact on how things sound. Make sure everything is properly balanced, and that levels are properly in check. Make sure everything can be clearly understood. We'll be talking more about all of this throughout the rest of this chapter.

Temporary mix

If your piece will be going to a mix session, then you have more room to vary in how polished and tight your temp mix is. Pick a general range for your average mixing levels and stick with that; -14 to -8db digital is perfectly fine for most non-final mixes.

If your mix is not the final mix, treat it like it's the final anyway. While it may not be wise to spend edit time in certain super-picky areas, the thought remains: **pay attention to details.**

Here's a secret: a lot of editors who know that their piece will be sent to a mix session become sloppy. They let clunky audio edits slide by, they let disjointed music edits remain unpolished, they let certain sections of dialogue remain difficult to understand. The train of thought is, "Eh, it's gonna be mixed, they'll fix it there."

Often if we can't hear something, the automatic solution seems to be "turn it up." This happens with dialogue a lot. But maybe you can't hear the dialogue because elements underneath it are too loud. If you already set your dialogue level, most times you'll want those levels to stay there. Don't arbitrarily raise them because other elements are louder. Instead, turn that other stuff down.

Maybe you've set your initial levels, and you have two sonically important elements competing with each other, but you don't want to turn either one of them down. Well, chances are your audience isn't going to fully hear either one if they're stepping on each other. In that case, consider adjusting the timing of when the elements stop or start.

Suppose you have an important song lyric that you want to have playing in a dialogue scene. The dialogue is still important, so find a way to have that important lyric drop in either during a pause in the dialogue or after the dialogue finishes. Otherwise you would have to mix it way down in level so it wouldn't compete, and then you might not hear it at all.

This book doesn't completely address everything on *any* subject. Having said that, discussing "mixing as adjusting relative levels" would be woefully incomplete without the number one tool to help that happen: audio compression.

AUDIO MIXING

RULE #49 | USE THE SECRET WEAPON OF COMPRESSION TO CONTROL LEVELS.

I don't use the term "secret weapon" lightly. Audio compression is a *crazy* powerful tool that's rarely used by anyone except audio engineers. But if you can gain an understanding of what it is and how to use it, your mixes will improve by leaps and bounds.

What is this compression thing?

Most editors hear "audio compression" and think of a digital method of squishing the amount of information contained in an audio file. That's not what we're talking about here.

This kind of compression is a way of controlling the difference between the loudest louds and the softest softs of whatever piece of audio you're compressing. When used subtly, you can barely tell that the compression is there – the only difference is how high the levels do or don't bounce on your audio meters. When used in extreme ways, you'll see the audio meters slamming up to a specific level like they're hitting a brick wall. And the sound that's being compressed will sound mostly the same as it did before… but it will definitely feel like something's reining it in, keeping it under very, very tight control. Extremely compressed sound feels like it's screaming right up in your face.

Why do people use audio compression?

Audio pros mostly use compression for dynamic control, making sure audio levels stay within certain desired boundaries. It can also be used to help certain sounds be extra crisp and clear, cutting through the clutter of whatever else might be there.

For our purposes mixing audio mixing for our editing, compression is HUGE for dialogue and voiceover. If people are whispering one moment and yelling the next, dropping properly adjusted compression on that clip of dialogue will smooth it out instantly, like magic. If you've recorded some voiceover tracks for your piece, dropping compression on your voiceover will make all the consonants crisp and clean, and the VO will just plain sound better.[39]

If you happen to be responsible for the final mix on your edit, dropping some medium-strength compression on your entire mix as a whole will smooth out bumps and spikes in your levels, plus let your entire mix sound fuller and louder... if that's what you're going for, of course. (Remember the Internet? Mix it LOUD LOUD LOUD. For this, compression can be your best friend.)

How it works.

Words fall woefully short when describing a sound-based process like audio compression. So here's an attempt at painting a picture of how it works, courtesy of Saint, my German Shepherd.

> Me: Hey buddy, wanna explain audio compression to people reading this book?
> Saint stares at me with a happy, blank expression.
> Me: Lemme rephrase. Wanna go on a walk?
> Saint: ARRRR!!! AHHR AHHR UHHRR!!!!

There is nothing in the entire world Saint loves more than going to the park to chase his favorite orange ball. When I take him out for a walk, he is absolutely thrilled. He pulls on the leash and just

---

[39] *Judiciously applied compression has been one of my secret weapons for impressing people with my own voiceover tracks on projects that I edit. Extra VO gigs have earned me a nice little chunk of money over the years. If VO interests you at all, it's definitely worth looking into.*

AUDIO MIXING

wants to go, go, go. I want him to stay next to me, so I pull back on the leash. When he sees a cat or something interesting and wants to slow down, I give a tug on the leash to say, "Let's keep going."

With audio, some pieces get loud quickly. They're like Saint straining forward to get to the dog park, and compression is me yanking on the leash to slow him down.

Now for the nitty gritty. There are five primary elements of audio compression: Threshold, Ratio, Attack, Release, and Output Gain. (There are other parts to it too, but these are the main ones.)

The threshold setting is the point of loudness where the compressor should pull back on the leash. The higher the threshold, the louder the sound has to be before the compressor kicks in. If the threshold is low, then the compressor will be yanking on the audio's dog leash constantly.

The ratio is the amount of pulling back on your audio done by the compressor. If you have a 3:1 ratio, your source audio has to be 3db hotter for your compressor to let the output audio play 1db hotter. If you have a more extreme ratio, like 20:1, your audio has to be 20db hotter for the compressor to let the output audio rise 1db hotter. Ratio is how hard the dog is pulling against the leash, and how hard I'm pulling back.

Attack is how fast this process begins. Sometimes you want the compression to be subtle so it can sneak in and sneak out. In that case you set it for a slow attack. Sometimes the audio gets loud quickly (Saint sees a cat in the neighbor's driveway and starts to freak out), and in a split second you have to yank back. In that case you set it for a quick attack.

Release is the opposite. It sets the speed at which the compressor relaxes its audio leash. Set it for however quickly you want the compressor to go back to normal.

Now when you have all these settings operating, sometimes the effect is that the overall output level of your audio goes way down. Like you're pulling on the leash so much that you've almost stopped walking. Here's where you have to remember that the point of compression is to control the audio levels, not to get rid of the audio.

So now we want to take all that sonically squished audio and turn everything up. That's Output Gain. The effect is that you have tightly controlled variations in how loud your audio gets and how quickly it happens or doesn't happen. In some editing software there is a box you can check that says, "Preserve Volume." That's what Output Gain does.

But let the mixer beware: remember that when you crank the output gain you are turning up ALL the sound in that compressed source audio. If your dialogue happens in a quiet place, fantastic, but if there is noise in the background that will get raised as well. And that will rarely sound good.

If this all sounds complicated, well… it is. Using compression well is a skill that has to be practiced to really understand what the compressor is doing, and why. But once you get the hang of it, your levels will stay strictly in line, and your mix will sound **BETTER**.

RULE #50 | SHAPE YOUR SOUND BY KNOWING AND USING EQ.

This is where audio mixers really pull out their bag of tricks. There is much that can be said about audio equalization, or EQ for short.

Mr. Hertz and his good vibrations

Audio is basically pulses of energy vibrating through the air in the form of sound waves. The lower the number of times per second that the sound waves vibrate, the lower in pitch the audio will

AUDIO MIXING

sound to our ears. The higher the number of vibrations, the higher the pitch. Audio folks refer to this as the sound's frequency.

A German physicist by the name of Heinrich Hertz decided to measure these audio vibrations. The world was so impressed and grateful that they named the actual unit of measurement after him – the Hertz, abbreviated "Hz." Building off Mr. Hertz's work, scientists determined that the human ear is capable of picking up sounds as low as 20 Hz, or 20 sound wave vibrations per second, all the way up to 20,000 vibrations per second. One kilohertz (1 kHz, or "1 K" for short) is 1,000 cycles per second, and 20 kHz is 20,000 cycles per second. So we say the human range of hearing is 20 Hz to 20 kHz.

What does this mean for our mix? Well, that 20-20k range describes the entire world of frequencies that you may or may not want to tweak during your mix. Boost a certain frequency or general frequency range – or remove a certain frequency range – and your mix will sound different, for better or for worse.

Trowel or paintbrush

Growing up, my older brothers both had portable boomboxes to play cassette tapes, CDs, the radio, or whatever they felt like listening to at the time. Always being the fiddling type, I loved to mess around with the oh-so-high-tech, 3-band EQ sliders to change the sound. These days, the sound system in your car very likely has an "Adjust Sound" option with options to boost or cut the High or the Low frequencies.

The above examples are examples of using EQ are about the same as an artist glopping paint onto a canvas with a trowel. It can get the job done in certain circumstances, but it ain't anything close to precise. The more you know about sound and how it works, the more precise you will likely want your tools to be. Instead of a glopping on sonic tweakage with consumer-grade, 3-band graphic EQ ("graphic EQ" is the kind of EQ adjustment with individual sliders dedicated to specific frequencies or frequency ranges), you might be more interested in the more paintbrush-like professional graphic EQ unit with 30 bands. You probably won't need one for our editing purposes, since professional graphic EQ units are most often used for the precise shaping of sound within specific acoustic spaces – for sound playback or live events.

Note: It's easier for many people to understand what a graphic EQ is and does compared to other more complicated ways of tweaking sound. That's why your editing software probably has some version of a graphic EQ function that you can use to adjust sound elements in your sequence.

And instead of shoveling on the EQ with a "boost or cut highs and lows" like your car system might offer, you'll definitely want to become familiar with the much more precise offerings of parametric EQ.

The parametric is your friend

Parametric EQ is powerful stuff, and like graphic EQs, it comes in varying levels of preciseness. Here's how it works: unlike graphic EQ, which only lets you adjust pre-determined frequencies, parametric EQ lets *you* choose which specific frequency you want to boost or cut… plus how many of the surrounding frequencies you want to take along for the ride.

In your editing software's EQ controls, you'll typically have some sort of virtual slider or knob that selects the frequency that you want to boost or cut. Audio folks usually refer to it as the "sweepable mid" – because your selectable range can sweep back and forth within the mid-range frequencies. Then you'll have the option of selecting your bandwidth (audio folks call it the "Q") – how wide or narrow a range of surrounding frequencies to be affected as your boost or cut your target frequency.

Then, for the top or bottom frequencies, your parametric EQ will use some version of what audio folks call high-pass, low-pass, or shelving filters. Sometimes you get to select the actual frequencies at which they operate, other times they're actually closer to what you have in your car with the "cut/boost highs or lows".

"Okay, this sounds nice," someone might say, "but how the heck does the stuff actually work?"

And that would be an excellent question; just like different kinds of editing software all accomplish the same basic purpose, graphic EQ and parametric EQ both accomplish the same purpose. No matter how many knobs and sliders you may have at your disposal, it's up to you, the editor-turned-audio-engineer, to figure out what you actually want these tools to accomplish. And for that, we need to talk more about sound itself.

Where does the sound live?

Here's the thing: to make good adjustments with EQ, you have to know which parts of sound live in which part of the audio frequency world.

The human voice, for example, is a complex blend of audio frequencies. Even though we regularly adjust the highness or lowness of our voice when we talk, the main "meat" of the human voice stays in generally the same frequency range; the sonic core of the female voice is in the middle of the frequency spectrum (audio folks call it "mid-range"), and the sonic core of the male voice is typically in the lower end of the middle frequencies ("lower mid-range"). This part of the voice is most often used when using vowel sounds in speech. Ahh, eee, ooh, etc.

EDIT BETTER

But that main core of the voice isn't the only part – we make all sorts of sounds with the use of air, tongue and lip positions that come out as the airy, percussive, or sometimes hissing sounds of the consonants in the words we speak. This stuff lives almost exclusively in the mid to upper range frequencies.

If one of your characters has a crazy lisp when he speaks, and you want to adjust the sound so his "s" consonants aren't hissing like a rattlesnake with PMSsss, you have to know where those hissing frequencies live in order to reduce them, or "roll them back." You can tweak the 100 Hz low-range stuff in his audio clips until you're blue in the face, but that hissing won't change until you adjust the right area of high frequencies, say 5-9kHz.

On the flip side, say you have a scene where somebody is restoring a classic muscle car, and they start it up for the first time. The recorded sound of the newly souped-up V-8 engine might sound good, but why not make it really rumble and roar? That won't happen by boosting the mids or the highs. Take that 100-300 Hz low range and boost it until the audio sounds beefy and powerful. Just don't boost it so much that your speakers blow up, or your neighbor thinks you're launching a spaceship out of your edit bay.

Tweak away: add and subtract

Just as with **RULE #48** (**Think of mixing as adjusting relative levels**), EQ can be equally effective by boosting specific frequencies ("making certain parts of the sound louder") or cutting specific frequencies ("making certain parts of the sound softer").

Maybe your source clips have a low, constant hum in them from an electrical circuit. If you live in North America, most of those electrical hums live at 60 Hz. (If you live elsewhere than North America, they may pop up at 50 Hz.) In that case, you can use parametric EQ set with a very narrow bandwidth to 60 (or 50) Hz, and cut that little slice of the frequency pie WAAAY back. The effect will be almost magical – that horrible, obnoxious low hum will have vanished, and the rest of your sound will be unaffected. The only reason this works as well as it does is because that hum has a very narrow frequency that's typically not in the frequency ranges we want to protect.

But more often than not, sounds you want to get rid of live in the same general frequency area as sounds you want to keep. That's where things get tricky. For instance, if you have dialogue or interview audio that contains music in the background, well… it's virtually impossible to completely get rid of through EQ. You might be able to make it less noticeable by cutting certain midrange and low frequencies, but it will never go totally away. Music in the background of audio has such a large range of frequencies that change from moment to moment that if you cut back every frequency in that music, you'd also be affecting pretty much everything in the dialogue that you want to keep.

Let's use another example of audio that needs some mixing love, say dialogue recorded outdoors on a windy day. That's often easier to minimize or maybe get rid of it all together.[40] Most gusty wind frequencies live in the lower range. Using EQ (graphic or parametric) you can cut back or "roll off" frequencies below 200 Hz as a starting point.

Now, if the person talking is a man, you have to be careful about how much of those lows and low mids you're removing. The sonic core of most male voices is in the 200 to 500 Hz world. If you take out too much of the low end for the wind, you risk taking away the meat of the male vocal tone.

---

40   And in that case, most audio professionals would approach it with noise reduction software before moving to EQ. But for the sake of conversation, I'm assuming that most editors won't have noise reduction software.

Female voices, on the other hand, are typically higher in pitch than males. So if you have rumbly wind and a female voice, you can take out frequencies all the way up to 300 or 400 Hz, you'll lose most of the wind sound, and you are still preserving the sonic core of the female voice.

If you happen to have a piece of audio that sounds unclear or muddy, that can come from having too much mid-range sound. Consider cutting some of those mids back between 500 Hz to around 2 or 3 kHz.

Sometimes you end up cutting everything *except* the mids – ever wanted normally recorded audio to sound like it's coming from a telephone? Telephones have very limited ranges of audio that they capture and reproduce, just what's absolutely necessary to preserve vocal intelligibility. So chop off the low and high frequencies and just leave everything in the middle.

EQ isn't all about cutting back frequencies; you will definitely want to add them too. We've already talked about the newly restored muscle car that sounds even beefier when you boost the lows around 100-300 Hz.

If someone on screen is hitting a punching bag, the same treatment might make more of a thump as the fist or leg hits the bag. If you don't care as much about the thump and you just want the "thwack!" to cut through your mix, give a boost to your upper mids and highs, say somewhere between 2-6 kHz.

And as editors, **one of the best general EQ boosts to use is that same upper-mid 5-9 kHz boost on dialogue.** Why? Because spoken words consist of vowel sounds and consonant sounds, and that upper-mid range is where those consonants live. People with great diction tend to enunciate their consonants very cleanly – boosting the EQ range that contains those consonants helps you to do the same thing with your mix.

AUDIO MIXING

A word of warning

Sound can be really, really tricky to mix well in a way that will work for any different situation. Bear in mind that sound is ultimately a very subjective thing that changes in a gazillion different ways. Here are just a handful of them:

- Mic placement and recording
- Formatting or transcoding of files during the editing process
- How clean is the audio signal chain in your editing system?
- How good are your speakers?
- What kind of acoustics does your room have?
- Do you have a cold, stuffed-up nose, or unpopped ears?

All this stuff affects how you hear and perceive sound, and if they're not all working together, your mix may end up sounding very different than you intended.

So if you really need your mix to be right on the money, do everything in your power to either be the kind of person who knows how to deal with all the above factors, or get it to someone who does.

COLOR CORRECTION AND GRADING

Color correction is a unique animal. It might seem to function sort-of-almost in the same world as general editing – because it's dealing with picture, right? And because my software has color correction tools in it, that means that anyone can do it and call themselves a colorist, right?

WRONG.

It's true that much of today's editing software has color correcting tools easily accessible to any editor. And it's quite possible to adjust color and make it look closer to what you ultimately want.

One might say the same thing with sound mixing – any decently advanced editing software has tools to help the general editor polish the audio, but those tools pale in comparison to the actual consoles, mixing set-ups, and **knowledge** used by audio engineers for a finished mix.

Beyond sheer knowledge, the visible tools of the sound mixer are the main reason most producers, directors, and clients generally understand that the video/picture editor is rarely the most qualified person for a polished sound mix.

But coloring tools are often built right into the editing software. And that's a huge reason why it's much, much less likely for a professional video editor to be asked to do a finished sound mix then for a professional video editor to be asked to complete a full color finishing pass. "The color correction tools are right here, why do anything beyond that?" producers and clients often say, *not knowing what they don't know* about what the tools and knowledge of a professional colorist can bring to the project. Or, they do know the value of a colorist and just don't have the money to pay for one. That happens a lot too.

Believe me, a professional colorist can talk most editors under the table when it comes to technical mumbo jumbo, creative applications of color, and dealing with giving high-maintenance creatives. (Hey, sounds like the Technician, Creative, and Psychologist Hats that we editors wear, huh?)

In the meantime, the editor is expected to know something about everything these days, especially color correction.

A beginning point: there's a difference between color correction and color grading. Color correction is the basic adjustments that get light and color levels into the general area where they need to be. Color grading is then the precise, creative decision-making that gives the piece a polished, specific look.

For us non-colorist video editors, our available tools can indeed accomplish a great amount of both color correction and grading.

COLOR CORRECTION AND GRADING

> **RULE #51** | **KNOW THE DIFFERENT LEVELS OF COLOR TOOLS AND WHAT THEY DO.**

The fundamental underpinnings of color correction get crazy technical really quickly, so I'm not even gonna go there. Sorry, no breaking down color space and 3D LUTs.

Just like sound exists on a range of low, mid and high frequencies, images range between dark and light, zero color to lots of color. For the sake of keeping things simple here, we'll focus mainly on adjusting those two things: light (luminance, or luma for short) and color (chrominance, or chroma for short).

In **RULE #50** (**Shape your sound by knowing and using EQ**), we talked about applying EQ with a trowel or a paintbrush. Well, it's the same with color correction, but maybe even more extreme – with detailed, professional adjustments being made with an artist's paintbrush, then decreasing amounts of painting detail with a 12" roller, and huge swaths of correction applied like paint with an industrial paint sprayer.

Basic Controls: The Industrial Paint Sprayer

Any basic color correction in your software will usually consist of controls that include brightness, set-up, contrast, hue, and saturation. This is the equivalent of applying color correction in big, sweeping strokes with an industrial paint sprayer. Here's a brief breakdown of the above controls:

• Brightness is pretty much what it says – adjusts the overall intensity of the picture's luma channel. Here's the danger – if you want to make the picture brighter, raising the "brightness" control or slider tends to raise everything else with it. As in, it raises the highlights, *and* the midtones, and even some of the dark levels if you're not careful. This is rarely the best way to adjust overall picture brightness – your picture will quickly start looking odd. Grey, milky, loss of detail, all sorts of funky things that you probably don't want.

- Set-up or black levels. Set-up is a now outdated term that refers to the reference point for black in analog video machines. Thankfully, the general editing world now only deals a digital scale of 0% luminance being completely black and 100% luminance being completely white.[41] Adjusting this control, like brightness, tends to affect the overall scale of luminance and usually messes with more of the mid-tones and highlights than is wanted. Having said that, *lowering* the set-up or black levels is more likely to look good, since that's one of the most often used functions of color correction to begin with.

- Contrast is a ratio between your brightest highlights and your darkest shadows. If you increase the contrast, that ratio gets more and more extreme until you end up with only full white and full black with no levels of grey in-between. At times, a high contrast image can look eye-catchingly good, though getting high contrast video to work well usually requires more tweaking than is possible with moving the basic "contrast" slider in your software.

- Hue is the balance between the different elements of color (Red, Green, and Blue, if you're working in an RGB color space). In fact, "hue" is often referred to synonymously with the word "color" in general. In basic color correction, adjusting the "hue" control usually does a huge sweeping adjustment of ALL the color in ALL the picture – highlights, mid-tones, and shadows. That's a recipe for making your entire image look sickly green or purple. Good luck with that.

---

41   Interestingly, the digital world does have percentages of "super white" that go above 100% luminance – kind of like getting extra credit and scoring 107% on a test in school, which is always fun, yes? Super white is used mainly for specialized graphics work.

COLOR CORRECTION AND GRADING

- Saturation is the intensity of the color in your image, and it's one of the most popular settings to fiddle with. It's also one of the easiest basic settings to tweak and actually achieve a good-looking, stylized result. Bumping up the saturation makes the colors pop out and become more vivid. Crank it up too much and the colors start bleeding into each other. Reduce the saturation slightly (and usually increase contrast), and you have the popular faded look that used to be possible only by running physical film through the bleach bypass process. Remove the chroma by complete desaturation, and ta-dahh – instant artsiness!! If you remove the chroma, all that remains is the luma… Black and White.

Intermediate Controls: The 12" Paint Roller

When I was in kindergarten, my dad spent some time as a professional house painter, both interior and exterior. For years later, he'd take on the random painting job here and there, and sometimes I worked with him. I learned all sorts of things about painting. For our purposes here, I will say: the classic paint roller can get a bunch of paint on a wall really quickly. It can also execute a surprising amount of detail work. Doing so might require more work than other detail-oriented tools, but it can be done. Hence my comparison of intermediate color correction tools to the humble 12" paint roller.

Most decently advanced editing software has 3-wheel-style color correction built into it, and that's one of the main differences between basic and intermediate tools. You'll see 3 sets of controls for shadows, mid-tones, and highlights, often showing up as three wheels of color. These allow you to adjust the hue offset or color balance for any of the three areas. Along with the 3 areas of hue offset, most software allows brightness adjustments for each area by either having gain sliders underneath each wheel, or having nearby controls for Set-up, Gamma, and Gain/Brightness.

- Set-up we've already discussed. In today's digital world, it basically means your black or shadow levels. You will often be lowering them, or "crushing the blacks" – dark, rich shadows are a very popular look in all sorts of visual media.

- Gain refers to the brightness of your highlights, your brightest white levels. If an image is sort of grayed-out in the brightest areas, you'll usually want to raise the highlights. Be careful though – crank the highlights up too far, and you lose detail in them. Then you're left with bright blotches of formless white. Sometimes you want that, many times you won't. So how to make the picture brighter while keeping the detail in the highlights, you say?

Ah, that's the great part. Most often colorists brighten or darken the picture not by adjusting the bright stuff at the top or the dark stuff at the bottom, but by working with the stuff in the middle.

- Gamma is a beautiful, beautiful control. It's the big brother to contrast but is definitely its own animal. Where contrast deals with the ratio of bright highlights to dark shadows, gamma is the mid-point between the bright and the dark. If you raise the gamma, then that midpoint between bright and dark rises, pulling the surrounding areas of mid-range up with it. **This makes the whole image appear brighter overall** *without touching the highlights.*

That right there is a big, big deal: being able to affect the overall brightness of the image without changing the highlights. Because if you go back to the basic controls and raise your Gain, Brightness, or Exposure controls, it pulls up the bright parts, the mid-tones, AND the shadows up with it, often in ways you don't want.

Avoid the "brightness" control and roll with the gamma, my friends.

So these intermediate color tools are more like applying paint with the 12" roller. You can get lots of things done, even get some detail work done. And I'll say that other than some visual plug-ins for creative color grading (film effects, vignettes, blurs, custom paint effects, etc.), these intermediate tools can take care of the vast majority of your non-mission-critical color work.

Candidly, they're the only tools I've ever used for my own coloring needs, because any piece I've ever edited doesn't need anything beyond them, or they need the highly precise correction and grading performed by actual colorists using the actual tools that colorists use.

Advanced Controls: The Artist's Paintbrush.

I remember the first time I sat in on a color correction session. I was a young assistant editor, delivering show elements to one of the many Hollywood post houses that no longer exist, and I was allowed to watch the session. I sat on the luxurious leather couch in the darkened color correction bay, snacking on the plate of fresh fruit and exotic cheeses especially prepared for us. I watched as the colorist fiddled with knobs and sliders on his spaceship-like console, occasionally picking up the phone to consult with his minions down in the machine room, all the while examining a mystifying collection of displays and making adjustment after adjustment.

Up until that point, I had seen the show dozens of times and thought it looked pretty good. But under the watchful eye of the colorist and his room full of specialized, intimidating equipment, the footage that I had been so used to seeing in its uncorrected state turned into polished, glossy television.

I was astounded. To this very day, I still shake my head at the amazing changes that can take place to a project under the discerning eye of a professional colorist. And not only is a professional colorist valuable for the creative input he or she brings, colorists also have a wealth of knowledge on the best way to output, display, and preserve all those detailed tweaks to your project.

EDIT BETTER

The details of the tools and techniques that colorists use, specifically for detailed color grading, are beyond the scope of this book. For our purposes, know that they include the basic and intermediate controls discussed above, and a whole bunch of things beyond.

> **RULE #52** | KNOW THE GENERAL TECHNIQUES OF COLOR CORRECTION AND GRADING THAT WILL HAVE THE GREATEST EFFECT ON YOUR PROJECT.

In the meantime, for us video editors tasked with the need to know something about everything, here are some of the general color-related tasks that tend to pop up and how to take care of them.

General color correction tasks

- **Correcting exposure**. If an image is too dark, raise the levels of the mid-tones or the highlights as discussed above – super easy. If the image is looking milky or hazy, that can usually can be fixed by lowering the shadows and adjusting the mid-tones. If the image is crazy bright all over because it was shot overexposed… well, that's tougher to fix. Most times if an image was shot with the highlights blown out to pure white, you've pretty much lost all that detail in the brightest part of your frame, and you're stuck with the results. Sorry.

Notable exception to this sad case: the more information your camera recorded to begin with, the higher the chance those blown-out highlights can be pulled back to reveal details that still remain. This is especially true if you shot on an advanced cinema camera with huge media files.

- **Match shots.** The most common issue with shot matching is mismatched color balance. Say you have a two-camera shoot, one camera's footage looks fine while the second camera's footage is blue. Well, assuming that the blue is a mistake (which isn't always the case), the fix is usually pretty straightforward. The bulk of that

COLOR CORRECTION AND GRADING

color balance lives in your mid-tones; in your 3-wheel color corrector, pull the center of the mid-tone wheel away from the blue towards the opposite yellow/red side of the wheel.

- **Correcting illegal colors**. Illegal colors, you say? There are laws about color? Well, yeah. In this case, it's not the government you need to keep happy, it's the anal-retentive broadcast engineers at television networks. Video formats allow you to tweak color and brightness to technical measurements beyond what most broadcast outlets will accept, hence the term "illegal color." So, what are these illegal colors and brightness levels? They depend. Recognizing and fixing them is one of the primary functions of professional colorists.

The main point for our discussion here is that most reasonably advanced editing software has some sort of limiter or "legalize color" setting or filter to drop on top of a sequence. If you have to deliver your edited piece to a broadcast outlet without the benefit of a professional colorist, that will take care of a bunch of issues that could otherwise give the network reason to kick back your piece to get fixed.

General color grading tasks

This is the part of coloring that can be really fun, and it's the place where professional colorists really shine. Grading is the part of the color process that creates or enhances mood or emotion through the coloring. It's also an opportunity to more fully tweak out the visual attention magnets by telling the viewer where you want them to look.

EDIT BETTER

Here are some ways for the non-colorist to accomplish typical color grading tasks:

- **"Make this video look more like film."**[42] This is a huge one, one of the most often-heard request in terms of color, and it's assuming you want it to look like modern, polished film instead of grungy, old film. If the request comes across worded like that, then the person asking probably isn't all that picky. What they usually mean is:

- **"Just make it look better."** Video is notorious for looking washed-out and having bland colors. Given those two things and our previous discussion, it's usually an easy fix: lower the shadow levels – also known as "crushing the blacks" – and increase overall color saturation. Often images will benefit from raising the mid-tones too.

This is as close as you get to an instant "make it better" button for coloring. For people who know they want a more specific look, that's easier to achieve than one might think:

- **Add a specific look or style**. This is where your coloring filters or plug-ins can save you a ton of time. (For those wondering, this is where LUTs – Look-Up Tables – come into play for professional color grading.)

Applying a Film Effect usually does the above-described color saturation and black crushing, but it will often give you more options too – adding grain, glowing highlights, or adding grungy elements like shake, lines, dust particles, etc. Speaking of grunge and aged

---

42   Important! Making video look like film happens in two primary areas: color and frame rate. This is not the book to go into the nuances of scan lines and engineering geekery. Suffice it to say: you can have the most filmic color grade on the face of the planet, but if your piece runs at an interlaced frame rate instead of a progressive frame rate, your piece WILL feel like video. So for the non-colorist editor who wants to "film up" the piece, experiment with settings in your software that let you de-interlace video, double up fields, or even add a 1-frame strobe to your shots.

film, if you want an old film look, the older you go, the more you'll want to increase the overall contrast. Early film had WAY less space between the brightest brights and the darkest darks. Also, older film often has large-sized film grain.

Just like people love a good pair of faded jeans, many love a faded, washed-out color grade. The most popular version is called Bleach Bypass, named after a specific chemical process applied to physical film. The result: increased contrast and desaturated colors. So given what we've already discussed above, you can absolutely achieve your own Bleach Bypass look by increasing contrast and... would you believe... lowering your overall color saturation. Or you can just drop on a Bleach Bypass filter. That works too.

Sometimes achieving a specific look is as simple as adjusting the overall color balance, usually in the same way as described for fixing mismatched color balances between shots – tweaking the midtone color wheel. Except in this case, you apply the green, blue, or gold leanings to everything in your piece.

RULE #53 | USE COLOR GRADING TO ADJUST ATTENTION MAGNETS.

Another primary function of detailed color grading is to direct the viewer's attention. As we discussed in **RULE #12 (Actively direct the viewer's attention)**, our brain gives weight to certain visual elements based on a complex hierarchy of priorities. Every attention magnet in **RULE #12** applies to color grading, so I'm taking the liberty of repeating them here:

General attention magnets

Imagine standing in an art gallery filled with paintings. Here's how your brain sorts what you see:

- In an otherwise blank space containing one single object, our eyes will be drawn to that object.

- If an image contains multiple unrecognizable shapes (say a grouping of straight and curved lines) and one very recognizable shape (the outline of a tree), our eye is drawn to the shape we recognize.

- If a black and white image contains one piece of color, our eyes jump to the color.

- When we see anything resembling a face, the focal point usually ends up being the face's eyes.

- If anything with a face is looking in any obvious direction, the audience's attention will be moved towards the same direction.

Now imagine leaving the gallery of paintings and walking down the hallway to another group of rooms displaying projected video images with accompanying soundtracks. We now have more magnets to add because of the moving video:

- Motion is the great trump card, one of the strongest attention magnets that exist. Our eyes are instantly drawn to motion over almost anything else.

- Motions that are accompanied by sound are more magnetic to attention than motions without accompanying sound.

- Picture trumps sound. Our brains rely more on what we see than what we hear.

COLOR CORRECTION AND GRADING

Additional attention magnets affected by color grading

• Given indistinct or blurry surroundings, our brains will focus on areas with the sharpest detail. Grading application: if a visual element is overly sharp, consider adding a subtle blur to it.

• Given a uniformly dark surrounding, any bright object will stand out. If that's what you want, great. But if a bright object is calling too much attention to itself, consider darkening just that object. Vice versa, if you're wanting to highlight something that's darker than it should be, consider brightening just that object.

• Given a bland or low-saturated color environment, intense color will attract more attention from your brain. If an intense patch of color is attracting too much of the limelight, consider desaturating it.

So how does one do these things? That depends on your tools – a professional colorist has all sorts of ways to select certain parts of the image to blur, darken, or selectively desaturate. Most editing software lets you do the same sort of thing by applying vignettes, blurs, or custom paint effects directly to the clips in your sequence. You can also take a copy of a video clip stacked on top of itself, apply your correction to the top layer, then create a custom matte to reveal the unaffected video on the lower layer.

These are only scratching the surface of how the Editor Who Has To Know Something About Everything can bring his or her piece closer to a place where it looks like someone actually paid attention to the color correction and grading.

But seriously, any time you get the chance to have your piece attended to by an experienced colorist, DO IT.

EDITING PROCESS

So after all these ideas on ways to approximate the polished work of professionals far more experienced in their own niches than we will ever be… here's a section that puts things squarely back in the court of you and me, the editor.

Here are ways to help us in how we approach the editing process.

RULE #54 | CHANNEL YOUR INNER HENRY FORD.

Even though Henry Ford lived and died long before picture editing became available to the general public, we can learn some important things about editing from him.

Before he came along, automobiles were made by craftsman who did every single task themselves.[43] These early vehicles took a long time to make and were very expensive. Ford saw this and thought, "This is not efficient. Why not have a whole bunch of people instead who each focus on just one task?"

So he started implementing this crazy new thing called the assembly line. One guy, for example, just puts on wheels. Put on a wheel, put on a wheel, put on a wheel, all day. At the time, people thought it was weird because no one was doing it.

But what Ford knew, and what we've since come to realize, is that the efficiency of the assembly line comes from the focus of process.

Editing works the same way.

Consider an assembly line process for your editing workflow. There are so many functions in editing - building the foundation of content, adding coverage, adding music, sound effects, mix, color correction, etc. - that it's temptingly easy to jump back and forth between tasks.

But it's that switching back and forth between tasks that's the killer.

---

43   *Huh. Sounds kind of like the modern video editor, yes?*

EDITING PROCESS

Constant jumping from one function to another dilutes your mental focus, and it *will* suck up your editing time. If you have unlimited time available to do your edit, then by all means flit around from thing to thing… if that's your thing. Otherwise use your limited time in the smartest way possible.

Stick to one function at a time. Do your foundation work, THEN coverage, THEN music, THEN titles, THEN audio, THEN color, etc. Don't try to do everything at once.

But does that kill creativity? Some people will say, "This is personal. You've got to do whatever works for you. Doesn't this assembly line thing take out all the creativity?"

Heck no.

On the contrary, focusing on a single process **promotes** creativity. When you focus on a specific task, your brain has the opportunity to focus mental energy in that specific area.

Nobody's saying you have to be that guy on Henry Ford's assembly line who did nothing all day but attach hood ornaments to Model T's. But at least consider how the assembly line's focus of process can help *you* stay focused and highly productive in your edit.

RULE #55 | ORGANIZE YOUR WORK PROJECT. ESPECIALLY IF YOU'RE NOT AN ORGANIZED PERSON.

The bigger your editing project, the bigger the issues you will have if all the elements live in random places. If that happens you'll soon be asking questions like, "Where was that effect clip? Where was that graphic?"

That ain't good.

Knowing where everything lives lets you concentrate on what matters: creative decision-making.

When editing, your brain has to constantly evaluate and make choices, and you're shooting yourself in the mental foot if you end up distracted by something as lame as "Which sequence should I be using?" or "Where did I put that cue of music?"

This goes for any project, whether you're working on it yourself or with others, but when you're working with multiple editors organization is even more important. It's incredibly frustrating and time-consuming to come onto someone else's project and not be able to see which is the current version of the edit or where the elements live.[44]

Organization can be as simple or detailed as you like.

You could literally have three folders in your project that say CUTS, SOURCES, and OTHER STUFF.

Depending on the assistant editors or company practice, multi-editor projects will often be set up with numbered folders as seen below – they're numbered because computers like to arrange things in alphabetical order, and the desired order of folder names is usually not alphabetical:

00   TOP OF PROJECT MISC
10   CURRENT CUT
Contains one folder with the actual latest versions of project sections or entire project compilations.

---

44   Though if you're in a scenario with multiple editors on the same project, you will almost always have at least one assistant editor helping organize things from the beginning. In that case, keep on the assistants to stay organized, and in the meantime, practice what you preach.

EDITING PROCESS

    20   OLD CUTS
    30   EDITOR
             - EDITOR 1 FOLDER
                  - Individual sequences in progress
                  - Old personal cuts
                  - Selects or lifts
                  - Graphic and title junk folder
             - EDITOR 2 FOLDER
             - EDITOR 3 FOLDER
    40   SOURCE

This could have a couple folders of clips, or it could be an immense subdirectory arranged by shooting day, subject matter, camera load, etc.

    50   GRAPHICS
    60   SOUND EFFECTS
    70   MUSIC
    80   OUTPUTS
    90   ASSISTANT WORK

Organize your project in such a way that anyone could come in and pick up where you left off. Even if it's your own project, you might get hit by a truck or something and someone else would have to finish.

How's that for uplifting? Life is short, folks.

RULE #56 | NEVER ANYTHING "NEW."

I can't tell you how many times I've come on to a show and they say, "Okay, this is the *new* version." And I ask, "When was that new version put up?" "About 5 months ago," they say, "and here's what's happened since..."

Ah. So the "new" version is now old. It is no longer actually new, hence its name is meaningless.

STOP NAMING THINGS "NEW"!!!

IT DOESN'T MEAN ANYTHING!!!

At best, the word "new" is only accurate until a newer version replaces it. And you have no way of knowing when that will be.

A corollary to this: labeling sequences "Latest Cut" or "Current Cut." Now, this comes from a good organizational place – making sure there's a *place* where you can always find the latest version of the project. But think about it – if you have more than one copy of your project file or sequence that are both labeled "Latest Version" or "Current Cut"… which one is right? You could even have a specific date in the name, but if someone other than you has to work with your project, how will they know that the latest date is always the most current version? Because that's not always the case.

Do have a current cut folder or bin. Preferably keep only one sequence or version of your edit in there. If there's more than one, make sure there's a clear way to tell which one is indeed the latest, greatest "use this one!" cut.

But do *not* label the contents of that folder or bin "Current" or "Latest". Because that will change. If you want to label something, "Old," that's fine. At least that's objective.

But for crying out loud, don't ever label *anything* "New."

RULE #57	ORGANIZE CONTENT ON SEPARATE AND AND CONSISTENT TRACKS IN YOUR TIMELINE.

You know those quotes that talk about "a cluttered desk is a sign of a cluttered mind"? Well, replace the word "desk" with "timeline" or "sequence."

EDITING PROCESS

Is it true? Is it true of you?

Don't matter none. True or not, you should know that plenty of directors, producers, and editors believe that a cluttered or unorganized timeline is indeed a bad thing. Plus, a cluttered timeline will be frustrating to any assistant, finishing, or online editors downstream of you.

If part of your job is to keep those people happy, why not make it easier on yourself by keeping things organized? Also, it keeps things easier for you mentally by letting you focus more specifically on great editing instead of hunting for which clips live where in the timeline.

A typical organization goes like this: General program content goes on layer one, or V1. Cutaways might go on V2. Subtitles, graphics, and lower third text clips go on V4 or V5. Effects layers stack up however high you need. These things can vary (see the next rule), but the main thing is to choose a plan and stick with it.

For audio, start with dialogue on channels A1-A4. Then sound effects on tracks A5-A8. Then maybe music on A7-A10 and beyond.

This helps keep things consistent as you edit, and it's one less decision to worry about. It also helps if your project is going to be mixed at an audio mix house, because it helps them as they set up their mix session.

It also helps you apply changes all at once in your offline edit.

For instance, if you had a bunch of interview clips and wanted to boost the audio on all of them by 4db, it would be really annoying to have to pick and choose those random clips peppered all over different audio tracks. Instead, if you had laid them out such that all interview audio lived on A1 and A2, you could make that one selection to all the clips in those tracks at once. Boom. Done.

Or, say you want to change the color correction on all of a specific set of b-roll clips. Well, if you lay out your timeline such that all those specific clips sit on V2 or V3, you can immediately see which clips need adjustment, select them all, and boom. Done.

You'll find much saving of time and frustration when you take a little extra time here and there to keep your tracks organized.

RULE #58 | ADAPT YOUR ORGANIZATION TO THE PARTICULAR PROJECT.

The examples I gave in the previous rule can and should change.

Beware of anyone who says, "All your picture must be on the bottom video layer no matter what."

Most people whom I've heard say that sort of thing come from an age where intimidatingly complex machine rooms full of expensive black boxes juggled signals for analog, linear video editing… while polyester-clad producers sprawled on a leather couch in the back of the edit suite snorting lines of cocaine.

> Editor: How about now? This work for you?
>
> Producer: [Loud sniff] Yep. That's… GREAT.
>
> Editor: Alrighty then.[45]

While producers and directors do certainly still sniff the occasional mind-altering substance on the weekends, the Golden Days of Excess in the edit bay are long gone.

---

[45] *This might seem like hyperbole. I assure you it is not, though the bulk of it happened before my time. Most of the big post houses where that kind of stuff went down have either gone bankrupt or been sold to companies who promptly stopped serving catered meals every day. Sigh.*

EDITING PROCESS

As are the days of needing all picture on one stream of video so your switcher can read the EDL.[46]

Here's something that I use constantly: I've done a lot of work on projects that alternate between on-camera interviews and other documentary sound-ups. The temptation is to put all picture on one video layer, but I found that putting the soundbites on V1 and A1-2 while putting all the soundups on V2 and A3-4 gave me a lot more flexibility. You can swap out soundbites and reshuffle soundups and B-roll a lot quicker than if everything was sitting on just one video layer, and sound was sometimes on this track, sometimes on those.

Unless you're working on a formula-driven project that keeps doing the same thing over and over, almost every project will be different. So seriously, adapt for your project in the way that's easiest for you.

RULE #59 | ACTIVELY BUILD YOUR BAG OF EDITORIAL TRICKS.

Editors who edit with any regularity will find themselves reusing certain elements in different projects. Those elements should all be saved in a separate file, bin, or folder such that you can take it along with you as you go from project to project.

Did you just spend hours making a great graphics build that you might be able to use again? Save that sequence, my friend. Even if you have to copy extra media or create a new work project, save it.

If you have sound effects you tend to use repeatedly, save them. If you have color correction effects you find yourself going back to often, save them, too.

Don't go hunting for the same thing over and over again… when you only need to do it once, save it, and reuse it whenever you want.

---

46 *Archaic editing jargon used today by Nobody.*

EDIT BETTER

RULE #60 | DUPLICATE YOUR SEQUENCE OR PROJECT FILE REGULARLY.

Always make copies of your sequences and work projects. Editing systems give us all sorts of capability of tweaking and experimenting, so seriously… save different versions of things.

A good general practice is to duplicate your sequence and save the old version at least once every day, usually first thing when you start. Some days, so many different changes happen to different sections of a sequence that I save copies of sequences 3 or 4 times throughout the day just so I don't risk throwing away alternate versions of scenes by editing over them.

It's really, really frustrating to be sitting with a producer or director who says, "Let's take this part here and put it together the way we had it yesterday," to know exactly what they're talking about because you already did the work, and then to realize that YOU have to cut that section again… because you didn't save that other version.

Here's something that helps me a lot during screenings with producers: when we watch down the piece and they give notes or things to change, I often just leave notes in the cut with markers or locators, whichever software I happen to be using.

Here's the key: **before I make any changes, I duplicate the sequence and leave the just-screened sequence exactly as it is.** Then I go to the new copy of the sequence and make changes to it. That way I won't ever mistakenly change or delete the markers or locators in the process of making the changes. And I'll always know what the notes from the screening were because they're all preserved in the older sequence.

EDITING PROCESS

RULE #61 | ALLOW TIME TO POLISH AT THE VERY END.

Many times I've worked on a project that stayed pretty much the same all the way through the edit; then at very end, someone suggests some small changes, and they add a great finishing touch.

Or maybe you take the extra time to watch the project down one more time, wrapping up a loose end here, tweaking a few frames there. And it does actually help.

But some times – especially if you're paid to edit on a deadline – a project's schedule is so compressed that it's all you can do to just get the thing finished, never mind polished the way you'd like. And that's a bummer.

Do everything in your power to allow time to add those finishing touches before you step away from an edit. Here's why – and these reasons may or may not all apply to you:

1. Taking time to polish shows the people who hire or oversee you that you care about your work, and you care about the project for which *they* are responsible. That shows them that you are on their side.

2. If you're editing for pay, showing that you care about your editing sets you apart from all the other shmucks out there who don't. Because just like any paid profession, there are all kinds of apathetic shmoes who just plain don't care and say so. Others won't actually say so, but still behave that way.

If you're reading this, I'm assuming you do not want to be one of those people. More on this later.

3. Putting the polish on your pieces helps **you**. If you're not the one delivering the final, finished version, polishing lets you see the edit in as close to finished state as possible. And if you actually are

working on the finished version, then even better. Ideally, you'll feel good about the result, maybe get some closure or warm fuzzies. And hey, who doesn't wanna feel good about their craft?

RULE #62 | SET A DEADLINE.

Deadlines force action, my friends.

Few things strike more fear into my heart than coming on to edit a project with no completion timeframe or airdate, because then the fiddling and tweaking will be endless. Without a deadline, you'll end up with The Zombie Project That Never Dies.

Even if you're editing a personal project, *set a deadline*. Perhaps you can plan to show it at a specific event. For example, if you are putting together a retrospective of your son's high school basketball career, decide to show it at the graduation party. Otherwise, next thing you know he's off to college, life gets in the way, and the project never gets finished.

Also, deadlines help you manage your time.

As in: "Whoa whoa whoa, if I knew the piece had to be done by lunch, I wouldn't have spent an hour sorting and marking through every single take!"

Or: "So, the episode delivers in three weeks, and I need to finish three sections of it. It's the end of week two, and I'm still in section one. Something's gotta change here."

This applies to professional or personal worlds – fewer things will kick you in the butt to make things happen more than a legitimate deadline.

EDITING PROCESS

And here's another thing – when in doubt, make the deadlines shorter rather than longer.

Remember that feeling of impending doom in school as you looked at a deadline for a lengthy paper three weeks away? Most times we say, "Eh, we'll get to it later," until that feeling of impending doom turned into outright horror the night before?

In the great tradition of students everywhere, you then stayed up all night long fueled by enough caffeine to disqualify an entire team of Olympic weightlifters, you busted out the paper, and it was done. Boom.

Well, what if you would have short-circuited that whole "this is gonna be bad, oh crap I'll never make it" thing in the first place by setting a preemptive deadline? You bust out the first HALF of the paper one night, bust out the second half the next night, get some sleep BOTH nights, and you're done.

Apply that to your editing, especially personal projects.

And now, the exception: if you're working on a long-term project, be it a movie, TV series, documentary, whatever – beware of approaching it like a sprint.

You will burn out.

Think marathon. Pace yourself. And still live by ambitious yet achievable deadlines. You'll be amazed how much you accomplish.

EDIT BETTER

RULE #63 | USE WHATEVER PIECES OF EQUIPMENT WORK WITH YOUR STYLE. YES, YOU CAN USE A MOUSE.

Editing is a process that involves tools. Instead of being limited to scissors and splicing tape, the tools involve computers, keyboards, all flavors of mouse, tablets, wrist wrests, fancy chairs, exercise bouncy balls, standing desks, you name it.

The aim is to do the editing. There are indeed a gazillion tools to get it done.

Use what works for YOU.

If you want to sit on a bouncy ball and use a touchscreen tablet to control your editing rig from the other side of the room, go for it. If it takes forever to navigate your software to the point where you're not getting actual editing done... well, you may want to reconsider your touchscreen-only stance.

Say you've been using a clunky old keyboard with tall keys for a few years, and you get a new computer. Your old-school, slightly angled keyboard is now replaced by a shiny new keyboard that sits flat on the table and is the approximate thickness of a credit card.

All of a sudden, your wrists start to get sore after a few hours of editing where they never used to. Only thing physically different? The shiny new keyboard.

Whack it!! Bring back the old clunky keyboard that helped you get the job done without physical pain.

And now I know there are some folks out there saying, "Yeah, bring back that keyboard... and get rid of the mouse too. *Real* editors don't use a mouse."

EDITING PROCESS

Ohhhhh boy. Another pet peeve of mine.

I know these people exist, because I keep hearing stories about them. Usually college professors who say things like "Real editors don't need a mouse" or "I'll give you your mouse back once you're done editing."

Let me clear something up here: anyone who tries to tell you that to be a "real editor" you have to do it without a mouse is WRONG. And tell 'em I said so.

Out of the hundreds of editors I've known and worked with throughout my career in Hollywood, maybe five or six of them used a device other than a mouse or trackball.

And none of them *ever* used only a keyboard.

Now for the record, every editor I've known who uses a graphics tablet instead of a mouse is *scary* fast at editing. I'm not saying correlation is causation, but the correlation is definitely there.

Personally, my approach is a blend of mouse with my right hand plus a highly modified keyboard layout that lets my left hand sit on the left side of the keyboard instead of the right as per most software defaults. I've never had a need to use a trackball or tablet.

MINDSET

Editing is a mentally driven undertaking represented by the way we wear the editorial hat of The Psychologist. The ideas in this section are rarely a ddressed in writings on editing, yet they are critical to editing well.

So here we go.

EDIT BETTER

RULE #64 | TRUST YOUR INITIAL REACTIONS.

Your initial reaction to a piece is the most real it will ever be for you. It's the closest you can get to being the audience, and every time you watch that sequence again, your objectivity goes down.

This rule is especially important with comedy.

One time I was editing a show about a group of guys who run a chainsaw sculpture business. A cast member got it into his head that a carved Tiki log was haunted, since it kept showing up in random places, but it was actually another cast member playing a prank on him. It was a fun little storyline, but unfortunately the episode was already long. My producer and I, after racking our brains for other solutions, decided we needed to take the storyline out to bring the show to time.

When I screened the episode for the executive producers, they were worried that the episode wasn't funny enough. I mentioned that we had cut some scenes for time, and the execs said – almost as an afterthought – that they might as well watch them. I showed them the haunted Tiki log scenes, and the execs *roared* with laughter. These guys normally would just nod politely and say, "Yes, that's funny," but here they were laughing out loud.

So it was a no-brainer that those scenes would be going back into the episode to "up the funny" as producers like to say. And after that screening, nobody ever questioned whether those scenes were funny. We all knew that the first time producers saw them, everybody laughed.

I had to keep reminding myself of that while my producer and I went back to the drawing board to figure out how to fit an extra storyline back into an episode that was already six minutes long.

MINDSET

Beyond comedy, make sure you're very aware of anything that you feel on a first viewing. If you get chills, or you feel a tear welling up, that's all important stuff to remember down the road. Do everything possible to keep those strong moments in the cut… when you've watched the piece 87 times, and your objectivity is nowhere to be found.

RULE #65 | EMBRACE LIMITATIONS. THAT'S WHERE CREATIVITY FLOURISHES.

Everybody loves to say you have to think outside the box. Well, sometimes you're not allowed to go outside the box, because that's what the project is.

I'm reminded of a time when I was in a graphic design class in high school. One day the teacher said, "The assignment for tomorrow is to come up with a logo, and five different versions of it." So the next day I brought my logo plus five to class, and the teacher said "Great! For tomorrow, take your best logo of the five, and do twenty more variations on that one." My classmates and I looked at each other in horror. How on earth were we going to do that? But the thing my teacher knew – and I have since come to realize – is that when you have limitations you are forced to stretch *inside* the box. Sometimes that's where you find the most creative solutions.

As of this writing, I recently ended my time cutting a show about mixed martial artists getting ready for high-profile Pay-Per-View fights. The show is literally about dudes hitting other dudes, every single episode. So we constantly have to make dudes hitting dudes fresh and original… *again*. But we've come up with some really creative approaches, and that would have never happened if we had not been stuck inside that box. Sometimes limitations are exactly what we need.

EDIT BETTER

Bruce Lee was famous for saying, "I fear not the man who has practiced 10,000 kicks once, but I fear the man who has practiced one kick 10,000 times." So either way, as editors, you and I win – if we're doing "10,000 kicks once" and cutting all sorts of wildly varying content, fantastic. It's a great opportunity to learn about lots of different things. But if we're editing the same thing over and over again, that's an opportunity to hone our craft by practicing that one kick 10,000 times. And focused application of repetitive learning propels us along our path towards mastery.

RULE #66 | TAKE RESPONSIBILITY FOR DETAILS.

If you are one of multiple editors on a project, it's sometimes tempting to say, "Oh, I don't want to bother with that detail. I'll let one of the other guys take care of it." The next editor sees what you've left in the cut, assumes you did so on purpose, and leaves the thing alone. Next thing you know, the project ends up with all sorts of loose ends that never get addressed.

Granted, sometimes it doesn't make sense to obsess over details – we'll talk more about that in a second. But if you become an editor who lets stuff slide, and other people have to take care of it, your reputation will eventually reflect that.

How do I know this? I say this from my years of being a senior/finishing editor on projects, cleaning up all the details other editors left behind. Editors who constantly let stuff slide eventually have a difficult time getting work.

Be someone who takes responsibility for details.

MINDSET

RULE #67 | KNOW WHEN TO STOP TWEAKING.

Here is the yin to the previous rule's yang, and the balance to **RULE #61** (Allow time to polish at the very end):

Any project reaches a point where more tweaking, fiddling or polishing is just that… needless tweaking, fiddling, or polishing. It will not make the project significantly better, and will very likely make things worse.

When you reach that point, STOP.

How do you know when you've reached that point? Well… sometimes the clock tells you. Sometimes other people tell you. Other times you just have to figure it out for yourself.

A side note to the idea of tweaking: often the tweaking doesn't come from us, it comes from people above us and requires us to continue seemingly endless fiddling and polishing.

In that case, it's true… it ain't up to us. But bear in mind that the more tweaking the project is subjected to, the less we will care about it. While this is normal, we want to do everything in our power to limit it. We don't want to get to the point where we're working on projects we don't care about.

That is a very dark, depressing place. Errgh.

EDIT BETTER

RULE #68 | **INVEST YOURSELF AND BE WILLING TO RELEASE YOURSELF AT ANY MOMENT.**

If you are working as an editor for another person, the number one thing you have to realize is:

It is not your show.

Even (and especially!) if you are the sole editor on a $100M movie, it's not your baby – someone else has ultimate responsibility for it. Similarly, if the project is your show and you are the boss, then you need to be open to constructive criticism, especially if it's from a credible source. We quickly become blind to our own work, and feedback is the only way we can escape that blindness.

You don't want to be the editor channeling their inner toddler insisting "Mine, mine, mine!" It's hard, because we have our favorites – our favorite scene, our favorite music cue. Ask us to change them, and our inner two-year-old becomes righteously enraged:

"That's the best part of the piece!! I spent nine hours on that section without so much as a bathroom break!! Waaaaaah!!!! MINE MINE MINE!!!!!" We have all been there. If you haven't yet, you will.

It is not "MINE!!" We share. We play nice. Grown-ups call it "collaboration." Experienced, confident editors offer pieces of themselves in their work… while realizing that **we are not our work**. When needed, we instantly detach ourselves.

But what if our creative playmates want to change our creative baby in ways that seem, well… lame? Wrong? Just plain bad? Sadly, this is yet another reality of creative life.

In that case, if the client, the director, or the showrunner says "change it", the project is ultimately putting their butt on the line anyway, not yours. And nine out of ten times, you should just suck it up and change it. Eat your Brussels sprouts like a good little editor and git 'er done.

Here's a secret weapon – the Jedi mind trick to flip the Bad Note on its head while still soothing your inner tantrum-prone two-year-old. Ask yourself, **"How can I address this note and still make it work editorially in ways I might not have considered?"**

To some, this might seem basic. I assure you, it is not. I edit in a city of grown men and women who have been editing for *years* who don't get this. They fight and scratch and claw to protect their own creative turf… that ultimately isn't theirs in the first place!

And even for those of us who do actively engage in editorial collaboration, it's shocking how the process can move forward. To this very day, I still find myself caught off guard in times when The Boss says, "Do it like *this*," I cringe inwardly, then put in the skull sweat to make it work editorially anyway.

And in the times that the project becomes better, I can know that I participated in that victory.

> **RULE #69** | IF YOUR VIEWERS SEE, HEAR, OR UNDERSTAND SOMETHING OTHER THAN WHAT YOU INTEND, **THEY ARE RIGHT.**

Effective communication requires a message, a sender, and a receiver. If the message is not received in the way the sender intended, then the sender has not done an effective job of communicating.

It's one thing to put out a complex or ambiguous message and to be okay with varied responses.

But when we have a specific message to communicate? It's easy for us to get wrapped up in something and say, "Well, this is what it means, and the audience just doesn't get it."

Or even better, "I am an arteeste. The leetle people don't understand my geeenius."

Review above loophole on ambiguity. Then get used to the fact that nine out of ten times, *it doesn't apply*. If the audience doesn't get it, you're not doing your job.

Why is it so tough for complicated stories to succeed these days? Volumes have been written already. For us as editors, though, here's what we need to know: Today's culture of instant gratification, instant access, and miniscule attention spans now dictate that the masses want stories that are simple. Obvious. Even stupid.

Here's why: **The confused mind says "no."**

I'm sure you've noticed – a lot of the content that can be found on TV, online, and even movies these days is, well, dumb. So much is nose-on-your-face obvious. No nuance or subtlety whatsoever.

As depressing as it may be at times to watch, it's even more depressing to edit.[47] But this is the state of today's society. Because if the audience becomes in any way confused or bored, they will change the channel or click somewhere else so fast it'll make your head spin. So it's more important than ever before to communicate clearly and powerfully so your audience says "YES." Or at least, "I get it."

To those who dream of bringing complex pieces of cinema, documentary, or other content to the world: It is possible. And it is fiendishly difficult to do well.

One of the main reasons: the people behind these pieces often

---

47   *Ask me how I know this. Sigh.*

never master the feat of repeatedly telling stories in a clear, completely understandable way. So it's no wonder that their big, complicated works are either incomprehensible, or riddled with more holes than Bonnie and Clyde's getaway car.

There is nothing to be lost – and everything to be gained – by mastering the ability to tell stories in a compellingly straightforward way.

That way, you'll have a finely tuned sense on how to ride the balance between leaving enough of the story out of the picture to engage the audience, but not too much that it leaves them confused and annoyed.

RULE #70 | THE PROCESS IS OFTEN THE POINT.

Personally, I'm the type who likes to measure twice, cut once. Plan things ahead, know exactly what expectations are, meet them, and boom. Done, moving on. I've gotten really good at that over the years.

Which is why I continue to learn the application of this Rule. As much as I love to have a fully polished edit drop into the timeline from the very beginning, that's often not realistic, or even wise.

If the Boss doesn't know what he or she wants, your first cut will *definitely* not be the final cut. And it's that process of revision that often becomes the most important part of the entire creative process. Depending on the project and the people involved, that process can at times be excruciating. Or it can be an absolute joy.

I find that the more I embrace the Process, the more often it becomes the latter instead of the former.[48]

---

48   And let's be frank here: sometimes the way to protect yourself from an excruciating process is to remove yourself from the people who make it so. I have found far too many people who are excellent at what they do and know what they want to spend ridiculous amounts of time with people who don't even attempt to get their act together. Life is short, my friend.

RULE #71 | MAKE YOUR TOOLS INVISIBLE BY KNOWING THEM INSIDE AND OUT.

I was once listening to a discussion by one of the staff rerecording mixers at Warner Brothers. He spends each day in a rerecording theater with an audio console that requires four people to run it. It's huge, stretching from one side to the room to the other. He said, "The bigger the tools are, the more important that you know them like the back of your hand to make them invisible."

Any craft comes in two stages: learning the tools, then applying them in the most effective way. This applies to playing golf, building custom motorcycles, and most definitely to editing.

The world is chock-full of information to tell you about the latest tools and gizmos to help you with your editing. A lot of it is important and valuable.

But always remember the difference between tools and the work they help bring forth. Most editing software accomplishes the exact same thing at the end of the day. I have studiously avoided talking about specific editing tools in this book, because if you're reading this, I assume that you are more interested in improving the use of whatever tools you already have. **Tools change constantly – the concepts of powerful storytelling remain the same.**

In building a house, the master carpenter wants to use a decent hammer. He needs to know all the ways to use that hammer. But the carpenter is not the hammer, nor is the hammer the finished product itself. The hammer is only one of many elements that assist the master carpenter in building a masterfully crafted house that will become somebody's home.

MINDSET

RULE #72 | ADAPT OR DIE, BECAUSE TOOLS AND PROCESSES CHANGE.

Most television and film editors in Los Angeles use one tool. It's a really good one, and I would estimate that 85-90% of anything seen on a television or movie screen (at least within the United States) is edited on the same editing platform, which as of this writing would be the Avid Media Composer.

Thing is, we humans are creatures of habit, and it's easy for us to get stuck in mental ruts. Even to the point of editors turning up their noses at anything that *isn't* Avid.

Some time ago I watched a presentation given by Michael Cioni[49] in Amsterdam on the future of post-production. He pointed out, "Europeans often speak three languages, but only edit on one system. Why?" He was proposing that forward-thinking post-production people learn to use more than one tool.

"Well," we notoriously English-centric Americans might reply, "why learn new tools if my current editing software works just fine?"

Truthfully, you don't have to. **But hush your complaining mouth if you get caught by change that you could've seen coming.**

How many times have we heard those sad stories of highly skilled typesetters and pressmen who spent years and years learning how to run the most complex, fancy newspaper typesetters and printing presses? All of a sudden the newspaper says, "We're doing layout on computer now. Good luck to you." Or these days, "We're going digital only. No more print." And those folks are out of a job because they only knew one tool.

---

49   *Michael is quite the guy. Very, very forward-thinking and innovative in blending technology with creative purpose. Look him up online and follow him. And for the record, he also speaks German.*

Examples of this abound. Americans decry the thousands of jobs that have been outsourced overseas. Los Angelenos wring their hands, weeping in their lattes about all the film and TV production "running away" to other cities. "We just want things to be the way they used to be," they moan.

Wake up, people.

Things have changed. Things will continue to change. Keep up or get left behind.

Behold, the crystal ball.

Here's a very Hollywood-centric prediction that I offer for your consideration. It's fantastic news for everyone outside LA and horrifying news for people here.

To expand on the runaway production thing: as of this writing, film and television production continues to leave Los Angeles because the infrastructure needed for production now can exist anywhere. Los Angeles production continues to be more frustrating and expensive than other places. Unsurprisingly, producers move their production dollars elsewhere. Shock.

In the meantime, post-production is experiencing the same thing. While Los Angeles continues to be home to the highest concentration of editorial talent in the United States, it's because of TV post, not film. These days anyone can cut a feature film on a reasonably powerful laptop anywhere they want. But turning around episodes of television within its time and budget constraints requires physical infrastructure – just like the old way of making movies required huge studio complexes.

Specifically, broadcast television cut by multiple editors for tight turnarounds requires the editors to physically show up at editing workstations that are physically connected to a central media server.

When technology advances to the point where those physical connections are no longer required, TV post-production will do exactly what film and TV production work is doing.
It's gonna spread out.

And people in Los Angeles will howl and complain!! They'll moan that Someone Should Do Something!! It's just not Right!! This state of affairs is Unfair!! WAAAHHH!!!
That time is coming, my friend. It's not a matter of if, it's a matter of when. All the more reason to hone your skills in telling your story powerfully, because any story that shoots a lot of stuff and whittles it down to less stuff needs someone to do that. And that's what we editors do. Our role won't be disappearing any time soon.

So this is very good news for you. It is very, very bad news for people who refuse to change with the times.

Keep an eye out, because it's coming.

RULE #73 | ENGAGE WITH OTHER EDITORS.

Let's face it, this job requires a certain kind of person who not only survives but thrives on spending lots of time alone in a room with a computer. Editors, in general, are not a very social group of people. Having said that, I have gained huge benefits from engaging with fellow editors. To this day, I walk into someone else's edit bay, they hit a keystroke, and I say "Hey, what did you just do?" They think nothing of it because they do it all the time, but as far as I'm concerned, it's elfin magic. So I learn something new. I love that.

Some of the best ways to improve one's own editing is to look at other people's editing, especially if you happen to be working on a project with multiple editors. Dig into those layers, see what the editor did and how he or she built something that's worthy of learning to do yourself. Save copies of what they do, make it your own, and use it.[50]

If you don't have other editors around you, consider joining an area Creative Pro User Group. You can also read industry magazines, websites like ThePowerEdit.com, or books like this one. Keep challenging yourself to grow and expand in your editing skills.

RULE #74 | PURSUE EXCELLENCE EVEN WHEN IT SEEMS LIKE NOBODY CARES.

We editors are in a unique position to see the results of how other people have done their work before us. We are more likely to recognize when people are slacking. We know when the camera operator didn't get the shot. We know when the audio operator didn't catch that one line. Because we're the ones who have to fix it.

Our reputation rises or falls based on the quality of our work. Often that work will not be out in the open until weeks, months, or even years after we've finished. The last thing I want is to leave a trail of producers cursing my name because I didn't pay attention to details. Sadly, it's happened, but it doesn't have to happen continuously.

Even if it's not clear what effect your work will have, be excellent anyway.

If the world had more people who cared about the pursuit of excellence, the world would be a better place. Let us do our part to be excellent.

---

50   There is, of course, a fine line between homage and outright theft. That line will vary depending on the project and the person whose work you imitate.

BEYOND THE BETTER BUTTON

It would be really, really nice to have a magic button on our computer keyboard labeled **BETTER**. That button, of course, doesn't exist. So people write books about how to make your editing give the impression that it does.

I once heard the word "integrity" defined as "giving no reason for anyone to point at something and say 'AHA!'"

While Webster might snicker at such a non-academic definition, I like it. I make every effort to apply it to my editing, and I know I've done my job well when the director, producer, or client says, "Yeah, everything in that piece just works," or even better: "You nailed it. No notes."

Awwww yeah.

To have an edit that accomplishes everything of which it's capable, speaking its intended message with power and clarity – *that* is hitting the **BETTER** button. And that doesn't come from the footage or the tools of editing. It comes from you.

As the editor, you *are* the **BETTER** button. All those thousands of choices you make combine to create the overall experience of a compelling work.

But that idea doesn't stop with our editing. The **BETTER** button is every bit as applicable to our lives outside the edit bay. We make countless choices every day of our lives, shaped by forces and rules, both external and internal.

This book is filled with rules, many of them generally acknowledged, others put forth by yours truly. Suffice it to say, I am certainly not the ultimate source of authority.

Oh, that word. Authority. Many people chafe at the idea of being boxed in by rules and externally imposed laws. Others who engage with the rules find paradoxical freedom and joy by living within them.

Make no mistake, we are always under authority. Even the most iconoclastic auteur is subject to it one way or another.

As editors, we always operate under the authority of some entity outside ourselves, be it the producer, director, client, studio, network… or the audience.

Those entities have all sorts of standards that they expect from us. Some expect Whatever. Others are happy with Good Enough. Still others expect Perfect, with results coming closer at certain times than others, but never actually reaching it.

But here's a question that requires yet another choice: who is the ultimate authority? I propose that it's the Audience.

I am convinced that the Ultimate Audience exists and holds final authority. This Audience does indeed demand perfection that we can never attain on our own.

Those who openly engage with the Ultimate Audience find themselves changed. Our stories build and evolve in an ever-unfolding journey that one day culminates not in a response of "No notes"… but an affirmation past all our imperfections:

"Well done. You honor my vision."

ACKNOWLEDGEMENTS

Gratitude. My life is overflowing with it.

To the countless collaborators, employers, and friends who contributed to the experiences that shaped this book.

To Gordan Blazevic, David Paprocki, and Stephen Busken for your stellar contributions to the visual presentation of this book. Thank you for your artistry.

To Craig Valine and his Mastermind cohort who expand my mind to new ways of strategizing, communicating, and growing, and kicking me in the butt to git 'er done. See **RULE #62 (Set a deadline)** and **RULE #67 (Know when to stop tweaking)**. Okay, okay!!

To Rachel Coleman, Erica Tuns, Micah Yost, and Ed Zimmerle for your time and valuable feedback. Application of **RULE #61 (Allow time to polish at the very end)**. Good, good stuff.

To Wes Llewellyn, Adrian Pruett, John Rausch, and Myndi Shafer for your experienced and generously offered perspectives.

To Matt Wilson for his expertise shaping my assorted writings and transcribed ramblings into a well-formed manuscript.

To Tom Nash, Rick Roberts, and Dan Weaver, whose actions on behalf of a broke, young film student in LA allowed him to not only actually break into the business but thrive in it.

ACKNOWLEDGEMENTS

To Judy Blank, who – instead of kicking me out of the control room – pretty much blew my high school mind by inviting me to produce a piece for an honest-to-goodness TV show… and to watch an edit session that used an incredible machine called the Avid.

To Nancy Movall, who suggested I do a video in the first place.

To Ed Zimmerle, who repeatedly explained how a video should be ABOUT something, and to beware of flying sheep.

To Mom and Dad, who – among a million other things – encouraged a geeky kid to practice piano, hook up that Casio keyboard to his computer, and shuttle through hours of VHS tape, even when everyone else would rather play basketball than shoot it. For driving me to the edit bay through sunshine, snow, and blinding fog when I was too young to drive. And then not freaking out when I said I wanted to drive myself out to California. I love you both.

To Dr. Ron Rushing, who made a comment one day in class about the two things that last forever. Not only did it stick in my mind, it has become my life mission.

To Chantel. I love you, and I love living life with you. The best is yet to come.

To the Ultimate Audience. I am your servant.

GLOSSARY

16: Short for 16-millimeter film, as in "They shot on 16." Super 16 is a variation of the same film size.

35: See "16". Super 35 is a variation of the same film size.

Avid: refers both to Avid Technology Inc. – a publicly-traded company founded in 1987 based out of Burlington, MA – and their flagship NLE product, Media Composer. The Media Composer is typically referred to as "the Avid," as in "They're cutting on the Avid" or "Avid is the number one tool for editors to learn if they want to edit projects that pay well." Avid is by far the industry standard NLE platform used around the world.

B-roll: Generally refers to cutaways or general covering shots, typically not the primary content of the piece. Comes from the days of optical film labs when lab techs would lay out sections of film alternating in checkerboard fashion between the actual physical A-roll and the B-roll.

Bites: Short for soundbites. Usually refers to a complete thought from a formally interviewed on-screen personality. The bite may be unedited or a full-on Frankenbite. As in, "we need to swap her bite for something stronger." Often misspelled as "byte."

Control Track: In physical videotape, a consistent electronic pulse at the beginning of each frame that keeps the playback electronics in proper sync and at the right playback speed. Similar in function to the sprocket holes on physical film which keep everything running smoothly.

Dailies: in general, refers to unedited source materials. More likely to be used in the context of scripted projects that have specific camera set-ups and takes. Originates from the film world when everything shot the previous day would be compiled and screened for the director, producers, and others. Occasionally referred to as "rushes."

DP: short for Director of Photography.

EDL: acronym for Edit Decision List. Typically refers to a digital file that contains information of all the starting and ending points of picture and sound sources within the edited piece.

Final Cut Pro: A popular NLE from Apple, often abbreviated Final Cut or FCP. Since its introduction in 1998, it has gained significant ground among video enthusiasts and independent filmmakers. Successive versions of the program continued to improve professional functions to the point where Final Cut began stealing professional market share from Avid. With its release of Final Cut version 10, known as Final Cut X or FCPX, many professional functions were stripped out of the program, and the user interface was significantly modified. While many independent users had no issues with the changes in FCPX, those changes alienated a large number of professional users. Many former fans moved away from using FCP towards Avid, while others moved to the increasingly popular Premiere Pro from Adobe.

Frankenbite: a combination of "soundbite" and "Frankenstein," the novel written in 1818 by Mary Shelley about a mad scientist who stitched together a monster from pieces of various human corpses. Popularized through reality TV shows who regularly construct soundbites with significant amounts of variance compared to what the on-screen character originally said or intended. When done well, the viewer can never tell that any words have been altered at all. When done poorly, an attentive listener can hear stray consonants or syllables at edit points, or vocal tones abruptly changing between edits.

GLOSSARY

Linear editing: in video, the process of electronically copying portions of source materials in sequential order to a compiled edit master tape. Linear edit sessions were usually planned out in detail because portions had to be laid to the edit master in a specific order and often had to end at a specific running length. If changes needed to be made to the edit master in a professional linear edit session, often the system's digital EDL could be adjusted to make that happen. Basic linear editing systems had no such luxuries. If you wanted to change something at the beginning, you either had to make a submaster (copy) of everything, losing video quality in the process… or you had to start over from scratch. After you stopped beating your head against the wall in frustration. Be glad the linear days are behind us.

Locator: in editing software, a digital reference point in a source or edited sequence, often accompanied with typed notes of explanation. Sometimes referred to as "markers."

Media: digital video or audio files referenced by editing software.

NLE: short for non-linear editing/editor. Usually in context of "Avid is the industry standard NLE platform."

Notes: written or spoken feedback on any given project. "Her notes were very insightful" or "The network loves the show so much they gave 9 pages of notes." Can also refer to individual sounds of music.

Non-linear editing: the process of assembling digital picture and sound sources by direct, random access. Also the classic process of editing film, except the source materials were physical, not digital, and were assembled physically.

Offline editing: in digital editing, the process of editing high quality media or sources at low resolution for the purposes of minimizing hard drive or server storage. Historically this was the only way non-linear editing could function, because computing power was not yet sufficient to capture and output full resolution, uncompressed video. Creative decisions were made at low-quality offline video resolutions, and finishing took place at uncompressed, high-quality resolutions in a linear online or finishing bay. As computer power progressed, high-resolution picture finishing began taking place on NLE workstations, eventually making linear systems completely obsolete.

As of this writing, offline editing is still common for broadcast television, especially in Avid-centric workflows. Hundreds of hours of media are accessed and stored at low resolution on central media servers (this minimizes need for continually expanding server storage and allows multiple editors to access the same pieces of media at once), then reconnected to high-resolution media for the finished product. In many film and video contexts, the offline stage is now skipped as editors work directly with high-resolution media from the very beginning.

Online editing: refers to the finishing process for high-quality, uncompressed versions of TV and video projects, though sometimes for film projects too. It is typically the stage where color correction and grading takes place. Online editing used to be the domain of complicated, expensive linear systems or supercomputer-driven workstations. But not any more. Online editing is usually a very technical, detail-oriented process after the bulk of the creative decision making has been finished in the offline edit. Online editing usually has nothing to do with the Internet.

Pilot: an initial episode of a TV series, usually paid for by a broadcast network in order to make a decision whether or not said network wants to order multiple episodes of the show. "The pilot got great reviews from test audiences, and the network is taking it to series."

Premiere Pro: a popular NLE from Adobe. Premiere has been a long-standing, less popular offering ever since 1991. It has gained popularity since widespread backlash from Apple's release of

GLOSSARY

FCPX. Premiere is gaining ground in professional contexts, particularly for its well-planned integration of After Effects (worldwide standard program for visual effects) and Photoshop (worldwide standard program for photo and graphic editing), two other hugely popular programs from Adobe. Premiere, After Effects, and Photoshop are the primary elements of Adobe Creative Suite, or CS for short.

Render: the process of pre-calculating complicated effects that would otherwise be too involved for the editing system to calculate and play back in real time. "Render breaks" used to be long enough to go out for a walk and grab a cup of coffee. No more… computers are too fast for that these days.

Screening: the event of playing the entire piece for an audience, usually decision-makers on a project. As in, "I need to get the cut ready for a screening with the execs tomorrow morning."

Sound-up: a particular moment of sound or dialogue that interjects other elements in an edited piece. In news parlance, it's sometimes referred to as a SOT, an acronym for "sound on tape."

Sequence: a compilation of editing decisions in an editing timeline.

Timecode: a sequence of continuous numeric codes that provides a specific, unique number attached to each individual frame of picture or sound media. I once heard the difference between control track and timecode explained something like this: imagine you're driving at a constant speed down a long, residential street with lots of identical houses next to each other. Every house you pass is like one frame of video that gets its own pulse of control track. Control track doesn't care which house it is, it just cares that there's a house there, one after another. Timecode is the same thing, except each house has its own special address.

RESOURCES

To learn more about powerful communication through video editing, connect with the author and like-minded individuals at:

ThePowerEdit.com

Youtube.com/user/thepoweredit

On Facebook, look for "The Power Edit on FB"

About the Author

Jeff Bartsch built his career editing television in Hollywood for clients that include ABC, NBC, FOX, Universal, Disney, ESPN, MTV, and many others. His commentary on editing and the entertainment industry has been featured in USA Today, TIME Magazine, the Associated Press, and multiple textbooks. He and his wife Chantel live in Los Angeles with a very happy German Shepherd named Saint.

Printed in Great Britain
by Amazon